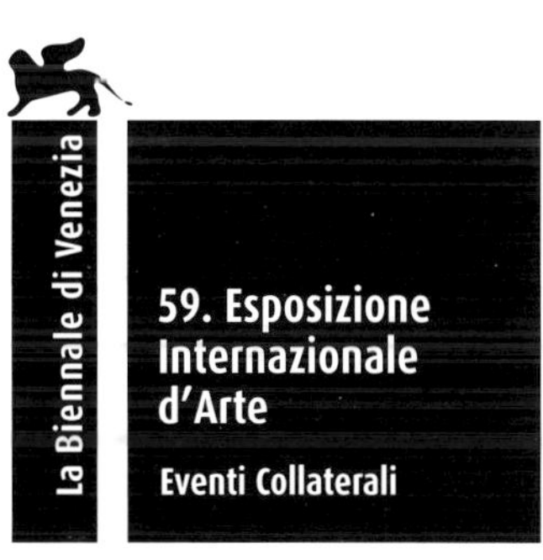

HA CHONG-HYUN

Kukje Art & Culture Foundation
Gregory R. Miller & Co.

TABLE OF CONTENTS

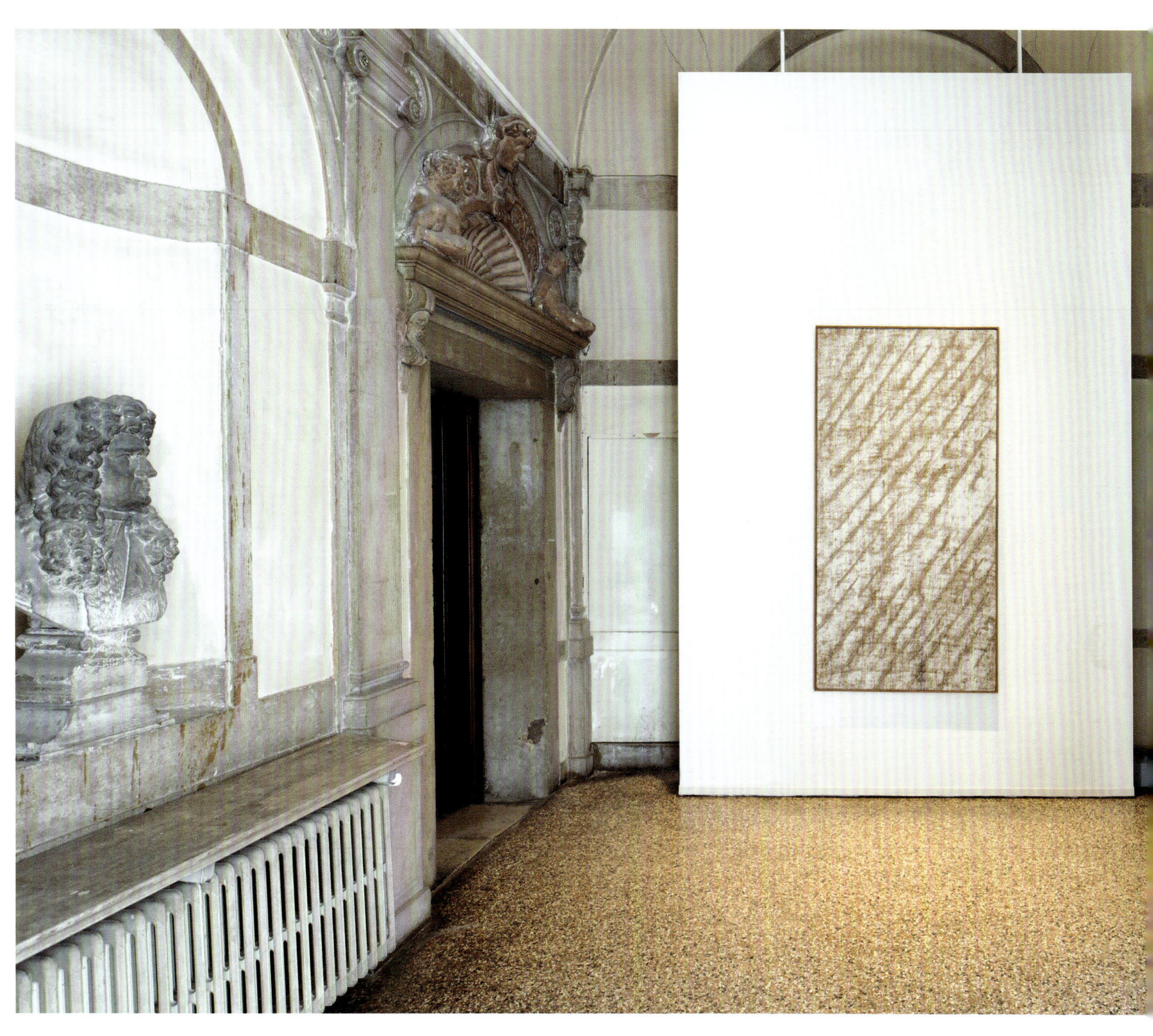

 Installation view of *Dansaekhwa*, Palazzo Contarini-Polignac, Venice, Italy, 2015.

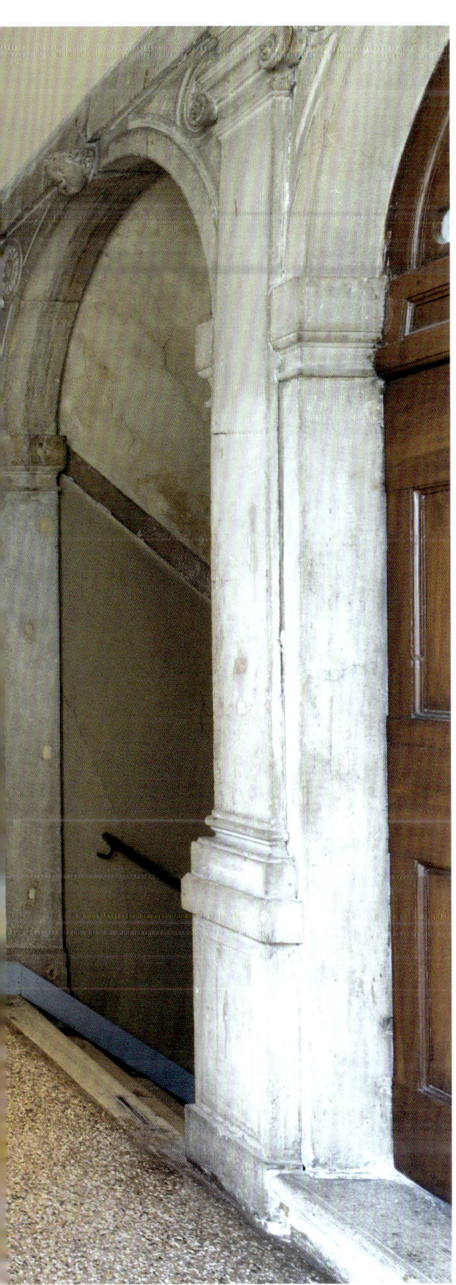

HA CHONG-HYUN

KIM SUNJUNG

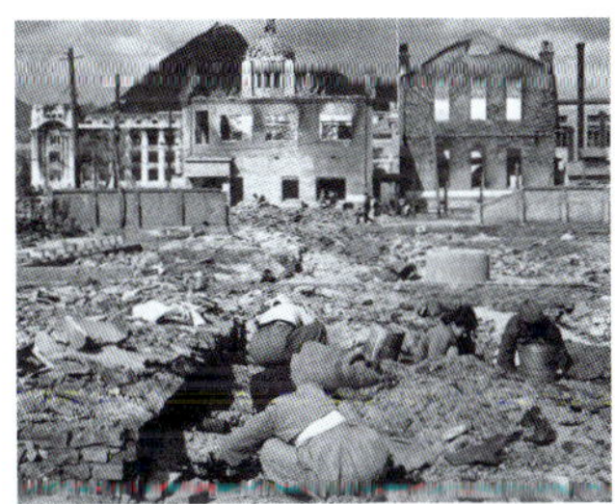

FIG 1

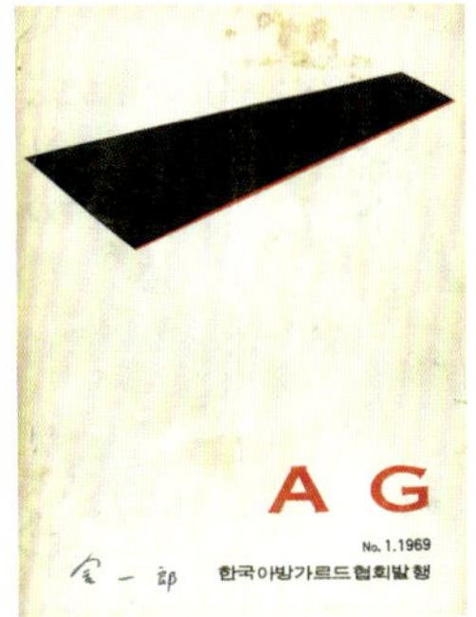

FIG 2

> Art speaks, and silence is a form of speech. In the art of Ha Chong-Hyun, unfolding for half a century now, I see both speech and silence with a strong kinetic energy.
>
> Kim Mi-Kyung, "The Art of Speech and Silence," *Wolgan Misul*, April 2008

Ha Chong-Hyun (b. 1935) is best known as a Dansaekhwa artist, but that designation applies to only one part of a varied practice that is devoted to exploration and understanding of materials and their physical and aesthetic properties. This retrospective exhibition features selections of the artist's work from the last sixty years and is intended to present the full breadth and variety of his materials and methods, as well as framing his ongoing passion for and commitment to creative experimentation. Surveying his oeuvre from his early abstract paintings and three-dimensional works through his latest *Post Conjunction* series (2008–2012), this exhibition also captures the artist's pioneering role in the development of "contemporary" Korean art.

Born in Korea during the Japanese occupation (1910–1945), Ha spent part of his childhood in Japan, returning to Korea after Japan's surrender in 1945. Following its liberation, Korea was divided in two, with the North overseen by the Soviet Union and the South by the United States, a schism that culminated in the Korean War (1950–1953). It was during the turbulent period of postwar reconstruction in South Korea that Ha was trained as a painter and emerged as a leading artist (fig. 1). After graduating from Hongik University in 1959, he produced abstract works that were linked to the then prevalent Korean Informel movement (see p. 46).[1]

But his distinctive use of dark tones, which he created by burning the canvas surface with fire, distinguished his works from the mainstream, evoking a powerful balance of aesthetic refinement and the bleak spirit of the time, an era still shadowed by the traumas of war. After participating in the Biennale de Paris in 1965, the artist shifted his practice, exploring Korean traditional decorative art methods, such as *dancheong* pattern and colors and mat weaving, and developed his own style of geometric abstract paintings inspired by the rapid urbanization of Seoul. Between 1969 and 1973, as a founder and active member of the avant garde artist collective known as AG (Avant Garde Association, fig. 2), Ha experimented with space by producing site specific installations and three-dimensional works with mundane objects, such as barbed wire, plaster, timber, metal springs, and newspaper. Recalling this period Ha has said, "At first I thought painting alone was not enough for me to fully express my thoughts, so I began to include a diverse array of materials in my works, which gradually expanded and led me to produce three dimensional objects with a strong experimental character."[2] The year 1974 saw the birth of the *Conjunction* series, which would make him a leading figure of Dansaekhwa, as he began pushing white oil paint through the weave of the fabric support from the back to the front.

With this new work, the young artist quickly rose to prominence, developing his own artistic vocabulary beyond the bounds of painting—a vocabulary

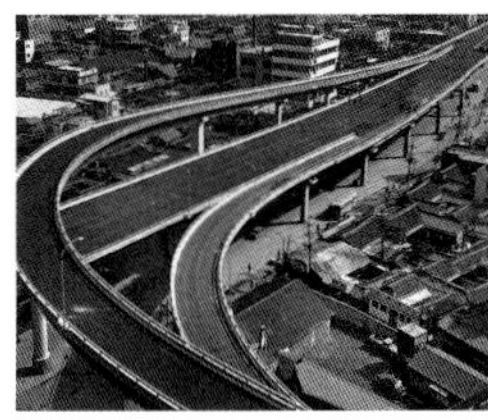

FIG 3

that reflected his broad interests in the contemporary social milieu. His experimentation during the early period of his career can be characterized by four tendencies. First, his work sought to comment on the bleak postwar sociopolitical changes under the military dictatorship using somber colors, soot, and found media such as newspapers, the latter implying the government's control of press and media. Second, the artist employed mundane materials, such as barbed wire, bent metal wire, and cast-off wood, attempting to connect his practice to the ordinary and the everyday. Third, trained as a painter, he made various attempts and experiments to overcome and challenge the two-dimensional boundaries of painting. Fourth, he constantly innovated with unusual materials and techniques he drew from domestic life and traditional crafts. Ha's breakthrough method used in his *Conjunction* series, which gained him international recognition, was an extension of his unceasing curiosity and experimentation.

This essay looks at Ha's oeuvre in five groups. The first group is his *Naissance* series and *White Paper on Urban Planning* series, which were the artist's focus between 1967 and 1968. The second conisists of works from his Informel years (early 1960s) and AG years (1969–mid 1970s), and his early *Conjunction* works (early 1970s). Then we will turn to the *Conjunction* series from the 1990s through the 2010s. The fourth natural group is Ha's *Post Conjunction* series (begun in 2010), and the fifth group to consider are recent works since 2020, including new works produced for this exhibition.

1 *NAISSANCE* AND *WHITE PAPER ON URBAN PLANNING*

After Ha's participation at the Biennale de Paris of 1965, he actively sought new methods and techniques, expanding his approaches to experimenting with the two-dimensionality of painting. Produced between 1967 and 1968, two new series, *Naissance* and *White Paper on Urban Planning*, show how the artist had developed his own geometric abstraction, drawing inspiration from Korean traditional arts and crafts and irregular patterns found in urban planning. In the *Naissance* series, Ha wove colorful strips of canvas into geometric patterns, as if weaving a mat with *dancheong* colors and patterns. *Naissance 67* (1967, see p. 49) is a canvas in the shape of a plus sign, consisting of a square canvas in the center and four equal-sized rectangular canvases attached like radiating arms; the woven straps of canvas in high-intensity colors not only comprise the picture plane, but also conjure traditional *dancheong* patterns. In works like *Naissance 67–A* and *Naissance 67–B*, the artist alternated woven patterns of squares and shapes resembling seeds, playing with the tension between geometric and organic forms as well as between two- and three-dimensionality.

Ha's production of the *White Paper on Urban Planning* series coincided with the rapid transformation of Korea from a war-torn country into an urban, industrialized one. While the government was aggressively carrying out its five-year development plan financed by the United States, the artist's abstract paintings recalled the newly constructed highways and beltways that were crisscrossing Korea. In *White Paper on Urban Planning* (1967), the upper half of the canvas is flat, but the lower half is literally folded, physically wrinkled like waves. The folds

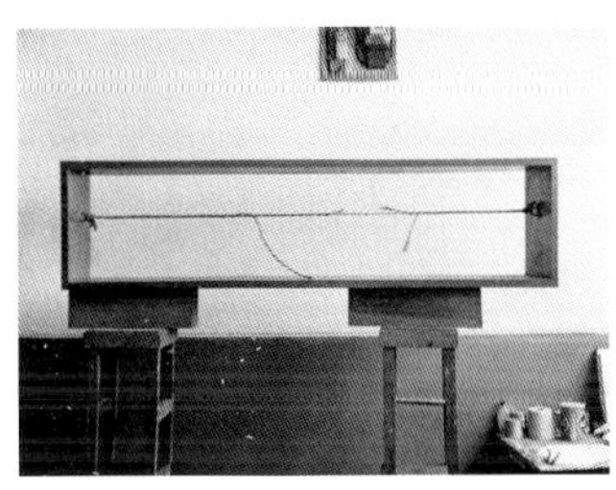
FIG 4

allude to the forced compression associated with the rapid urbanization and industrialization of Korea, as if representing a psychological and physical reaction to the sudden radical changes confronting the nation, or the experience of "a twist of time and space."[3] *White Paper on Urban Planning No. 1* (1967) suggests the sprawl of urbanization from the center to the periphery, and the bright colored diagonal lines in *White Paper on Urban Planning 68* (1968) deliver the striking impression of newly built highways (fig. 3). Responding to Ha's hopefulness about reconstruction, Lee Yil (1932–1997), the influential art critic who was close to the artist, called the series a "return to Constructivism," and is also known to have suggested the title for this series.[4]

2 INFORMEL, AG, AND EARLY *CONJUNCTION*

Ha's earliest work that garnered critical prominence was a series of abstract paintings that were linked to the Korean Informel movement. What distinguished his works from those of his peers was his distinctive use of dark tones evoking the somber atmosphere and social traumas that persisted in the postwar society. To produce *Work C* (1962), Ha applied thick layers of oil on the canvas and burnt the surface with fire to create shadowy patterns. *Amulette-A* (1963) contains a three-dimensional form made of a lump of thread, which the artist painted in oil and then burnt with fire. In *Untitled A* (1965) and *Untitled B* (1965), Ha combined methods of oil painting and collage on the canvas surfaces.

Having started to engage with diverse methods and materials in order to escape the two-dimensional bounds of painting in the above-mentioned *Naissance* and *White Paper on Urban Planning* series, in 1969 Ha co-founded the artist collective AG. Comprised of art critics (such as Lee Yil, Oh Kwang-Su, and Kim Bok-Young) as well as twelve artist members, the collective organized four exhibitions and published four issues of the journal *AG* (June 1969, March 1970, May 1970, and November 1971) over the period of its four active years.[5] Aiming to create "an art movement that builds a theory around a single logic," AG paid attention to the larger world outside the picture plane, which meant experimenting with space and commenting on the military regime metaphorically in their work.[6] It was during these years that Ha produced the installation *Work 71-11* (1971, fig. 5), juxtaposing a stack of blank sheets of paper next to a stack of newspapers he had collected for a year, which can be read as his response to the government's strict control of the press. Presenting tension and precarity simultaneously, the installation *Relation 72-1* (1972, fig. 4) consists of a rectangular wood frame in which a rope, pulled taut from opposite sides, suggests tension and an imminent break. *Work 72-7* (1972, fig. 11) is a roll of toilet paper cut into half, thus deprived of its function, evoking the impotence of society under oppression. These works were site-specific installations, and unfortunately remain only in photographs and documentation. An archive section at the entrance to the exhibition displays materials related to AG's activities, with a focus on Ha's involvement.

Of the diverse objects that Ha has worked with, his use of barbed wire has drawn particular attention. In the early 1970s, the artist produced a series of works by attaching barbed wire and wire springs to fabric supports in various ways, thus transforming and transgressing the supports' two-dimensional surfaces and structures, a gesture that art historian Kim Mi-Kyung has described as "trans-flat surface" (*talpyeongmyeon*).[7] In *Work 72-C* (1972), horizontal strands of barbed wire bind a white canvas. Almost like its negative double, the same-sized *Work 72-007* (1972) was produced by applying paint over barbed wire–attached cloth and then removing the wires, leaving only their traces. These two works together recall the relations between presence and absence, between the past and the present. In *Work 72-1 (A)* (1972), Ha pressed wire barbs into a fabric support, and in *Untitled 72-3 (B)* (1972) he covered his canvas entirely with coiled springs, letting a cluster of the bent spiral ends dangle in the middle of the canvas. On Ha's use of barbed wire, Philippe Dagen has written that the wire "encloses and pierces the canvas as if imprisoning and harming a body. As barbed wire unfolds from one end of the canvas to another, an aura of oppression spreads . . . taking on a political character associated with concentration camps, prisons, raids, martial law, sentencing, and war. . . . which does not mean that they are explicitly so. . . . the symbol is obvious: it has to do with a pain that does not make a spectacle of itself, but nonetheless expresses itself in a minor mode."[8] In a country that had experienced colonization, war, and physical division all within just fifty years, barbed wire quickly become a mundane, ubiquitous material. And with it, Ha made metaphorically powerful expressions.

It is interesting to note that *Work 73* (1973, see p. 59), in which Ha drew attention to the rear side of the painting support by attaching barbed wire onto the back, hints at a beginning of the *Conjunction* series, which he developed in 1974 by pushing lumps of white paint through the weave of the fabric support from the back to the front. To facilitate the movement of oil paint, the artist used coarsely woven hemp rather than cotton. In early *Conjunction* works (see p. 69), the artist used burlap sacks in particular—a choice that reflected his continued interest in banal industrial materials—retaining the burlap's natural color and texture in the final works.[9] After applying dense oil pigment onto the back side of his fabric support, he used blunt tools like a wooden spatula to push it through. This unique method has been referred to as *baeapbeop* (背壓法), literally translated as "reverse press technique." Kim Mi-Kyung has linked it to the Korean traditional painting technique of *baechaebeop* (背彩法, "reverse coloring technique"), used in Goryeo Buddhist art, for which colors are applied on the reverse side of paper or silk to render them semi-transparent on the front.[10] As Kim has put it, Ha "treated his canvas like an object in space and worked from both its front and rear sides."[11] In this way he completely freed himself from the boundaries of painting.

3 *CONJUNCTION* 1990S–2010S

The *Conjunction* works produced from the 1990s through the 2010s show a myriad of variations and the artist's endless creative experimentation. Brushing over the canvas surface after pressing paint from the back, Ha created countless different textures and trace gestures by using paint and variable brushwork on the variegated surfaces. The art critic Kim Bok-Young described Ha's *Conjunction* pieces from the 1990s as manifesting a "vortex of materiality" as the artist began to bring his "body and action to the fore" to be conjoined with the physical properties of the materials.[12] While the artist primarily used white paint in his early *Conjunction*, in the 1990s his palette expanded to include ochres, dark greens, and blacks, which were used monochromatically. This exhibition features selected white and black *Conjunction* paintings in particular. *Conjunction 92-24* (1992 , see p. 80) exemplifies overall compositions in black. (Some works that do not appear here, like *Conjunction 95-021* (1995) and *Conjunction 04-(B)* (2004), show looser compositions with black and white marks that appear to conjure calligraphic letters or urban landscapes.) *Conjunction 98-203 (A) (B) (C)* (see pp. 84–85) is a triptych in black impasto.

In late 2014, Ha began a new experiment with fire, a medium he had employed in his Informel works in the beginning of his career. He burnt a wooden stick wrapped in cotton cloth, applied the ash powder onto a canvas painted in white, and then scraped the burnt surface off of the canvas. On this method, the artist has said, "Spreading or pushing the singed paint forward, I see unexpected and peculiar colors emerge. In trying to embody and compress the depth of time in my work process, I've borrowed the power of fire."[13] Ha's interest in the compression of time was already evident in his *White Paper on Urban Planning* series, discussed above. As such, we can see the elements and experiments from his early work reappear and evolve later in his career. *Conjunction 17-96* (2017) and *Conjunction 17-84* (2017) demonstrate continued inspiration from traditional Korean arts, as the artist adopted the crimson color historically used in the exuberant *dancheong* and the ultramarine familiar from Korea's beloved *hanok* roof tiles. Composed from the bottom of the canvas upward, as if defying gravity, these works retain and manifest the resistance of his body and movement.[14]

4 *POST CONJUNCTION*

Ha's *Post Conjunction* works between 2010 and 2012 were produced by pressing paint between wooden shims wrapped in canvas and placed on the surface, causing the paint to be pushed through the gaps—a method employed in his work of 1974, *Work 74-A*, that used Korean *hanji* paper rather than canvas. In the *Post Conjunction* series (see pp. 110–11), the artist varied his colors and material properties. Not only did he use white plus various colors of paint for pressing, but the support could also be prepared unpainted or painted in color prior to the process. Ha also began works that used mirrored panels, so that the complex surfaces reflect the audience and their environment; additionally, he began to utilize collage on the surface of a canvas after pressing paint from the reverse side. In this way, within the parameters of the series, Ha has deployed a vast array of techniques exploring the support itself, the surface, and the physical properties of materials, including paint, gravity, and gesture.

5 RECENT AND NEW WORKS

This exhibition presents selections from Ha's new work produced since 2020. Ha produced these paintings by pressing white paint through the weave of the fabric support that was painted black, and he then further worked on the surface with black or other single colors. *Conjunction 22-01* (2022, see p. 103), for example, shows blue paint over the white paint pressed from the back, thus conjuring an image of sky. *Conjunction 21-74* (2021), in which black and gray oils coexist with the white oil emerging from behind, evokes the ink-and-wash paintings of mountainous landscape by the preeminent Joseon-period painter Jeong Seon. But Ha's works capture something beyond ink-and-wash watercolors; produced through an intensive layering process and by wrestling with his chosen materials, these works embody the artist's deep deliberation on the physical and aesthetic properties of paint and time.

From the beginning of his career, Ha has never stopped experimenting, constantly challenging the status quo and innovating with his materials and techniques. Living through the most turbulent times in modern Korean history—witnessing Korea's liberation from Japanese colonization, the division of Korea and the Korean War, South Korea's economic and industrial development, and the military dictatorship—the artist developed a practice that engages with both disappearing Korean traditions and the rapidly changing patterns of everyday life, one that is based on his lifelong study of materials and commitment to challenging the status quo. Surveying Ha's oeuvre from his early Informel and AG years through his latest works dated 2022, this exhibition hopes to capture not only the artist's endless creative and experimental energy, but also his pioneering role in the development of "contemporary" Korean art.

1 According to Lee Yil, "contemporary" art in South Korea emerged after the war, especially with the so-called Informel, an "expressionist abstract art movement" led by young artists. Lee Yil, "The Formation and Development of Korean Contemporary Art," in *Return and Spread in Contemporary Art* (Seoul: Youlhwadang, 1991), 91–92.

2 Lee Geun-Yong, "Material Meets Material," *Wolgan Misul*, July 1997, 128.

3 Kim Hyun-Suk, "Ha Chong-Hyun's Time and Space," in *Seventeenth Lee Dong-hun Art Prize Awardee Exhibition: Ha Chong-Hyun* (Daejeon: Daejeon Museum of Art, 2020), 38.

4 Lee Yil, "On Ha Chong-Hyun's Exhibition," in *Ha Chong-Hyun* exh. cat. (Seoul: Myung-Dong Gallery, 1974), n.p.

5 The *AG* journal played an important role in introducing contemporary Western art theories and artists like Marcel Duchamp, Lucio Fontana, and Christo to the Korean artists. The journal published Korean translations of writings such as Lee Ufan's "Introduction to the Phenomenology of Encounter: To Prepare for a New Art Theory," a major theory of Japanese Mono-ha. Lee Yil, a critic member of AG, argued that "avant-garde" includes Dada, Surrealism, American formalism, Neo-Dada, such as Jasper Johns and Robert Rauschenberg, and conceptual art, but not Social Realism. See Kim Jeon-Hee, "Study of Avant-Garde in Korea's AG Group," *The Korean Journal of Art and Media* 15, no. 4 (2015): 89.

6 Oh Sang-Gil, "Interview with Seo Seung-Won," in Oh Sang-Gil, *Re-Examining Korean Contemporary Art II* (Seoul: ICAS, 2001), 92.

7 Kim Mi-Kyung, "The Art of Speech and Silence," *Wolgan Misul*, April 2008, 173.

8 Philippe Dagen, "Ha Chong-Hyun, Concern and Silence," in Kim Bok-Young et al., *Ha Chong-Hyun* (Seoul: Misoolsarang, 2001), 187–88. Dagen's essay, originally written in French, was translated into Korean and English for the 2001 publication. For the version that appears in this essay, the English translation was edited by this translator.

9 In his interview with *Space* magazine after receiving the *Space* Art Prize in 1975, Ha said, "As you can see here, it's burlap sacks, and I pushed white from the back." Ha Chong-Hyun, quoted in "Interview with Ha Chong Hyun, the Recipient of the *Space* Art Prize 1975," *Space*, September 1975, 60.

10 Kim Mi-Kyung, "Energy Flow Time Void: The Discourse on Ha Chong Hyun," in Philippe Dagen et al., *Ha Chong-Hyun Retrospective* exh. cat. (Gwacheon: National Museum of Modern and Contemporary Art, 2012), 43.

11 Kim Mi-Kyung, "The Art of Speech and Silence," 172.

12 Kim Bok-Young, "Ha Chong-Hyun's Conjunction: From Conception to Development," in Kim Bok-Young et al., *Ha Chong-Hyun* (Seoul: Misoolsarang, 2001), 19.

13 Kim Hyun-Suk, "Ha Chong-Hyun's Time and Space," 40.

14 Song Mi-Kyung, "Ha Chong-Hyun: Physical Properties That Think," in *Seventeenth Lee Dong-hun Art Prize Awardee Exhibition: Ha Chong-Hyun*, (Daejeon: Daejeon Museum of Art, 2020), 18–20.

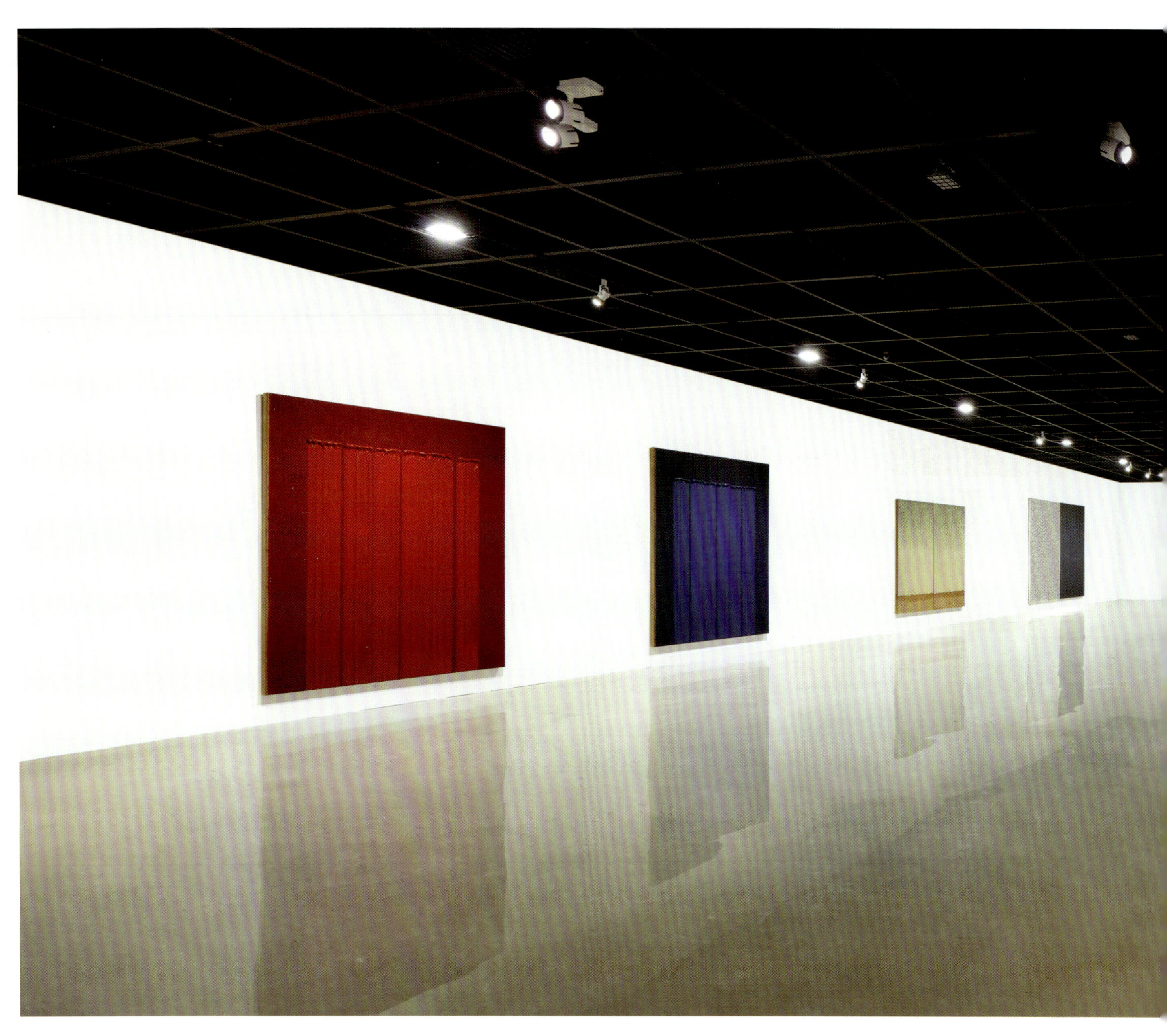

 Installation View of *Ha Chong-Hyun*, Daejeon Museum of Art, South Korea, 2020.

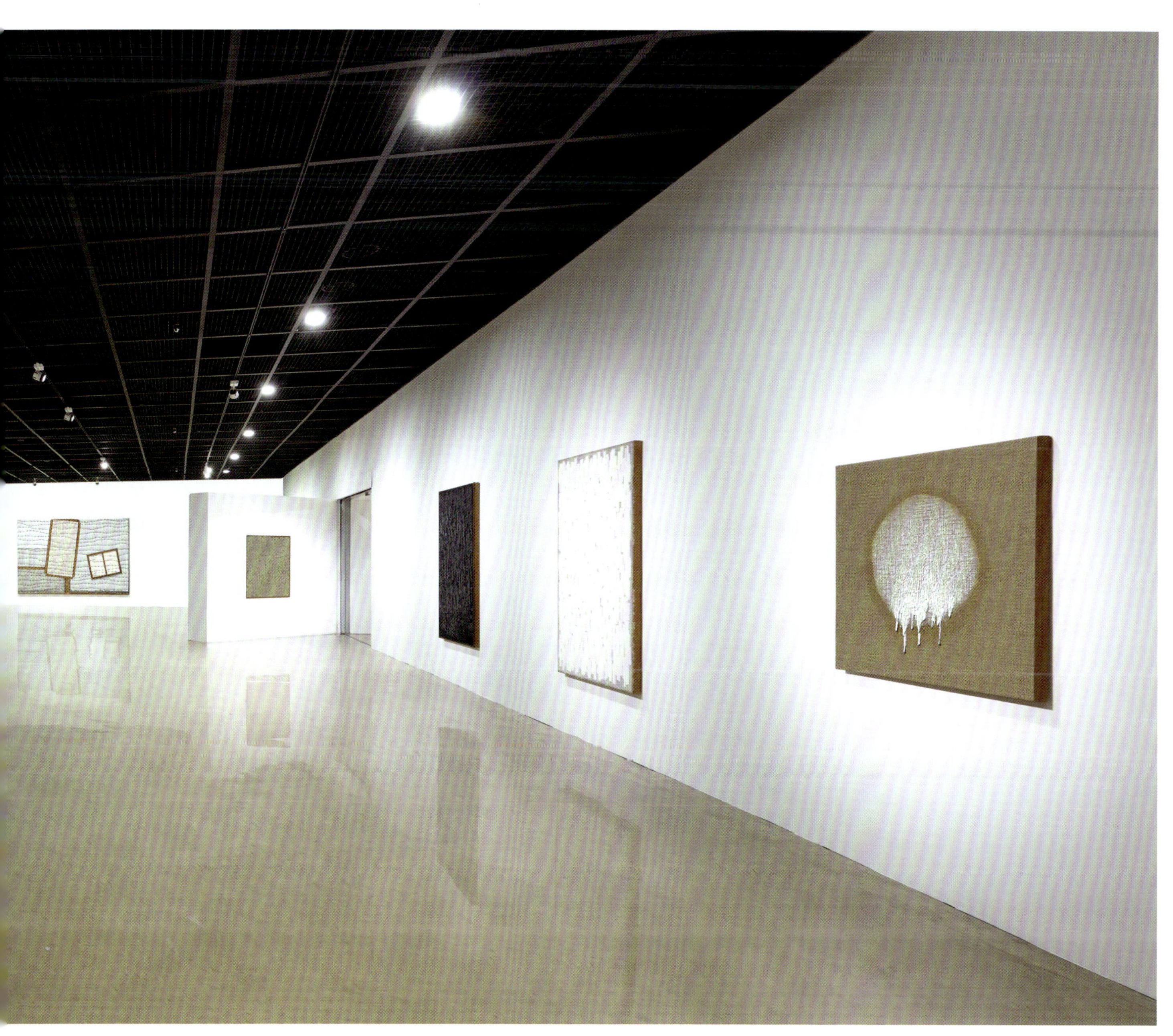

To approach and unpack the practice of an established, senior artist, who lives outside Western art capitals of the world, has for too long been tied to their position in relation to an assumed idea of a universal trajectory of modernism, locating their work within dichotomies of Western/Eastern, modern/traditional, contemporaneity/belatedness, and thereby overdetermining their works in relation to national or cultural identity. These dichotomies have only reinforced hierarchies implicit in Eurocentric readings of art history, and it is this myopic tendency that has prevented more complex art historical interpretations of non-Western modernisms. In recent decades, with new scholarship, research, and curatorial projects on international art histories informed by post-colonial theoretical frameworks, we have begun to acknowledge the pluralities of modernism in its different forms, temporalities, and pivots. This essay is informed by this wider lens of possibility and these intersecting and overlapping lines of the local and the global.

In 1992, Tate Liverpool hosted one of the first presentations of Dansaekhwa outside Korea. The exhibition, titled *Working with Nature: Traditional Thought in Contemporary Art from Korea,* was co-organized by the National Museum of Modern and Contemporary Art in Seoul. Though Ha Chong-Hyun did not participate, it featured several of his contemporaries, including Chung Chang-Sup, Yun Hyong-Keun, Park Seo-Bo, and Lee Ufan, many of whom came to be known under the term Dansaekhwa, or Korean Monochrome painting, as it was more commonly called then. The exhibition aimed to capture a shared sensibility using the theme of nature. Lee Kyung Sung, director of the Seoul museum, framed the question of the exhibition's aim this way:

> To ask oneself how Oriental thought has influenced modern art as a whole is by analogy to enter the relationship between contemporary Korean art and the rest of the world. . . . It is really difficult to define the word "Oriental." However, Oriental thought stands in opposition to Western thought, based as it is on intuition and irrational philosophy. In other words, union with nature is sought as an ideal. Unlike the usual practice of the Western world, where one tries to overcome nature by confronting it, the basis of Oriental ideologies is to blend in with nature and become a part of it.[1]

If the use of the term "Oriental" seems anachronistic in today's parlance, the positioning of these artists and their practices in the early 1990s, before the term Dansaekhwa was widely used, reinforces these dichotomies—of Eastern thought and Western rationalism; the natural and the artificial; the "Oriental" and the modern, while the curious framing of their works under "nature" seems unattuned to the sociopolitical context of their making. Curator Lewis Biggs located the origins and cultural context of the six contemporary artists featured, citing the formal traditions of Korea as deriving from Confucianism, Buddhism, and Shamanism, while attempting to negotiate these ancient philosophies in the practices of the artists against the backdrop of the massive urbanization of Seoul during the 1990s.[2] The Korean critic Lee Yil's contribution to the catalogue offered a more nuanced relationship, arguing that while Korean Monochrome painting is both "post-formalist and post-materialist, . . . one could be under the impression that the development of contemporary Korean art has imitated that of the West and America. For example, the terms 'Informel' and 'Minimal' are used in both contexts. But these labels are used only for the sake of convenience." Lee went on to explain, "Korean art at its inception was influenced by Western art movements. Having struggled to free itself from the impact of the West, modern Korean art's development has not just been a one-sided accommodation. Through these struggles, Korea has modified modern art to suit its own circumstances."[3]

A closer reading of the oeuvre of any of the individual artists in question can help free us from the one-sided limitations beset by negotiating terms and terminologies and the tendency to generalize and summarize, while allowing a more complex reading of an individual's practice on its own terms and within its own lines of trajectory. It is in this spirit that the work of Ha Chong-Hyun demands to be read.

Born in 1935, Ha received his art training at Hongik University, a place that would remain important to him in terms of his teaching,[4] as well as a site of temporary installations and conceptual works. At a moment when Korea was coming out of a devastating civil war that divided the Korean peninsula—a Cold War border that remains intact to this day—Ha graduated with a degree in painting in 1959, choosing to remain in South Korea for most of his life and career thereafter. The 1960s and 1970s were formative decades for Ha, both in terms of his involvement in the founding of the AG (Avant Garde Association) in 1969 and in his exploration of a visual language that led him to a wide-ranging and diverse body of works. It is important to note that during these decades, despite contemporary Korean art being relatively dormant on the international stage, Ha was participating in various biennales around the world—including the second Paris Youth Biennale in 1961, the fourth Biennale de Paris in 1965, the São Paulo Bienals in 1967 and in 1977, and the third Triennale–India in 1975—among others—while also actively showing in Korea. His involvement in the AG group demonstrates a practice and reflects a social context that were both keenly attuned to American and European art developments of the time.

While Ha's artistic contributions have been associated with Dansaekhwa and he is seen as one of its key protagonists—a legacy that has been resuscitated by recent exhibitions and scholarship—I would argue that his work and practice have always kept a conscious and wary distance from the tendency to be grouped in any totalizing art historical movement or oversimplified in relation to Western art developments, as he aimed rather to negotiate and eke out a distinct painterly language within the Korean context that is both universal and locally rooted. This is especially evident in Ha's early paintings from the 1960s and 1970s and the various styles he embraced before undertaking his signature *Conjunction* series.

Ha's interest in the changing physical landscape of Seoul and the radical transformation that Korea was going through during this time are demonstrated in a body of work he developed in the mid-1960s. Before adopting the pared-down, minimalist aesthetic of the *Conjunction* series, Ha was actively engaged in a painting practice that brought the outside in.

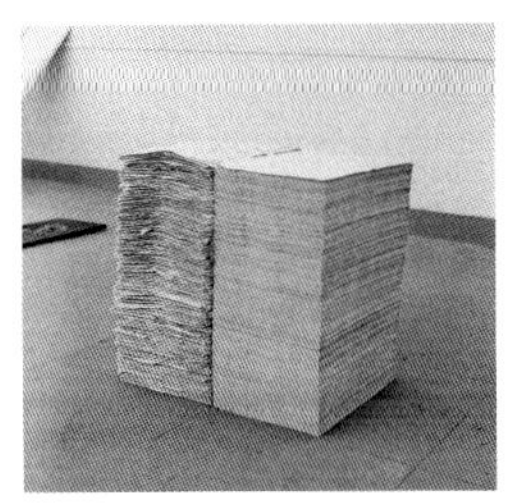

FIG 5

Through a highly abstracted language, he referenced the many changes to the landscape, having witnessed its transformation from a primarily agricultural area to an industrializing modern city. Under president Park Chung-Hee's autocratic regime (1961–1979), Korea went through a period of rampant modernization and industrialization with sweeping economic policies that aimed to project the nascent nation into the modern, developed world. His policies were both revered and defamed. In works titled *White Paper on Urban Planning* (see p. 53) made during the late 1960s, Ha created constructed abstract landscapes in which blocks of color and intersecting forms overlap on the picture plane. Defying the orthogonal grid and the rational mapping of city planning, the forms and lines of the paintings twist, turn, and move on the plane, creating a sense of flux, disorientation, and multi-dimensionality. He took this even further by folding the painted canvas, creasing and pleating it to create an accordion-like effect, thereby turning the painting into a relief and the flatness of the painted surface into three-dimensional space. If the banal title references bureaucratic mechanisms of urban planning, Ha's response seems to point to the collapsing of one reality into another. Whether read as a critique or a reflection, Ha's paintings seem to signal shifting forces and overlapping realities in tension with the bureaucratic efficacy promised by the title.

Ha's fascination with the city and its urbanization is addressed by art historian Kyung An, who describes these paintings as creating mandala-like patterns and having a relationship to traditional Korean culture. She writes, "The painting's formal elements hark back to colors and compositions found in Korean folk artifacts and architecture. For instance, the variation on the five cardinal colors of red, black, white, blue, and yellow strongly evokes *saekdong*—a rainbow or striped arrangement of vibrant colors found in *hanbok* or *dancheong*—decoration on traditional wooden buildings."[5] This is perhaps even more evident in the series *Naissance* (see p. 49) that Ha was painting around the same time. This title references a birth or origin, taking the relationship between Western painting and Korean culture even further. Using a color palette based on *saekdong*, Ha created tightly composed abstractions made up of repeated geometric forms. Here the color gradations move harmoniously from cool shades of blue to a warmer spectrum of orange and red. Quite unexpectedly, areas of the painted canvas are cut into strips and then woven together, forming grid patterns that resemble basketry on the surface of the work. In doing this, Ha not only integrated the traditions of Western painting with Korean *saekdong*, but also collapsed the boundaries between design, craft, and painting.

Ha took another turn in his painting practice when he started working with barbed wire and metal springs in 1972 (see p. 61). These works range in scale from modestly sized square canvases to larger horizontal landscape formats. What these works have in common is the use of the panel as a support structure to stretch lines of barbed wire or arrange coiled springs across the surface. At times, the barbed wire punctures the canvas and wraps around to the back of the frame as if confining or suppressing the physical limits of the work. The symbolism of the barbed wire, and the hemp fabric that appeared a few years later in the *Conjunction* series, was significant for Ha, who said in an interview:

> I used the barbed wire and hemp fabric, which I could easily find in the divided Korea, to represent my experience through the 1970s. They symbolize imprisonment and the profusion of military bases. I basically used stuff that was used in the war. Normally, hemp isn't readily available, but after the Korean War in 1953, there was no rice, and the U.S. brought in grains held in these hemp sacks to store. U.S. soldiers also rolled up the hemp and sold it at the Namdaemun Market [the oldest market in Korea]. I remember removing the remaining grains and bringing the hemp cloth home. The biggest size available was about 100 by 80 cm. So I couldn't make a large painting even if I wanted to. The work was a product of necessity and limitations.[6]

While these works have been read in the context of post-minimalism and Arte Povera in their use of "poor" materials, Ha's insistence on finding a painterly language utilizing the materials at hand speaks to his interest in the conditions of Korea during the 1970s rather than formal attributes of color and material. The prevalence of American military bases in Seoul was a stark reality of the post–Korean War order. If Park's economic policies during his oppressive reign created bold modernizing urban projects, those came hand-in-hand with the political and military realities of a monitored, undemocratic state, of a country wholly dependent on its ties to the United States. Ha's paintings negotiate these opposing realities, creating a visual language that not only upturns the conventions of Western painting but communicates the oppressive sociopolitical conditions that people found themselves in. His works at this time took a decidedly somber turn, with their lack of color compared to earlier works and use of untreated canvases and discarded metal. In their cold and harsh materiality, they can be read as stand-ins for the confinement and suppression of the body in a militarized society.

Ha's ongoing move toward non-conventional art materials would culminate in the *Conjunction* series, where he used loosely woven hemp cloth as the support of his paintings. These works are characterized by unconventional processes of pushing oil paint from the back, leaving marks and traces of white paint on the front side of the painting that Ha would then work and manipulate. The first of these paintings from the mid-1970s had the effect of a wash with the paint sitting on top of the unprimed surface, reinforcing the materiality of both the paint and its support in equal measure. He would find endless variations, introducing forms resembling horizontal bars or diagonal lines, or patterns of drips and daubs, then gradually introducing color and increasingly dense and intricate patterns like cross-hatchings. These works all carry the same title—*Conjunction*—followed by a numbering convention that begins with the year of their production.

Reflecting on the use of hemp, Ha stated in a recent interview:

> I used these hemp canvases to free myself from Western influences. I abandoned the traditional canvas because it was a support used in Western painting. Oil paint, brush, canvas—if I used these materials, the work would have been mostly Western due to its material origin and I wouldn't be able to articulate myself. Western critics have a bad

habit of trying to fit me into a Western category and comparing me to Western artists based on simple formal parallels, so I used hemp cloth to add complexity and make things more difficult for them.[7]

While Ha's response is clearly informed by the reception of his works and those of his Dansaekhwa peers in more recent years, Ha's practice was always predicated upon a deep insistence on painting as linked to the realities of everyday life—to the materials he found in his urban environment—to the scarcity and poverty of the times, and the "necessity and limitations" of society during the difficult and turbulent decades of Korea's social and economic development. While his works, like those of other Dansaekhwa artists, were inherently anti-expressionistic, they profoundly captured the will, desire, and commitment toward defining an aesthetic of the times.

While Ha remained skeptical of the label Dansaekhwa to describe a group of artists who shared certain tendencies and ways of painting in the 1970s, he also found the term convenient for signifying a specifically Korean context and defining it on its own terms. He stated:

> Western critics examine my methodologies and materials with an unfamiliar eye. They study our methods within the context of their own art history and try to look for similarities. This leads to the use of *Monochrome* and other familiar terms, and we must consider whether we find this usage appropriate. I believe we cannot allow the West to name a Korean creation. It is indeed a somewhat unfamiliar name to us, but the works we do and the name Dansaekhwa share a certain tone and character. Compared to Monochrome, Dansaekhwa is a far more suitable term as it describes a far broader spectrum. Considering this, unless a more suitable substitute emerges, this is the term that best captures the numberless hours our artists have invested. Having said this, we need to devote ourselves to a full-scale inquiry on this matter. The profound question of what defines Dansaekhwa must be answered and established internationally.[8]

Ha would continue to carry the *Conjunction* works forward into the 1980s, yet another tumultuous decade, beginning with the 1980 Gwangju Uprising and Massacre. At a time when the activist political art of Minjung dominated Korean art discourse, his commitment and integrity toward a consistent painterly practice somehow seem to best convey what Yoon Jin-Sup described as the "spirit, tactility, and performance"[9] at the core of Dansaekhwa. What Ha and other artists associated with Dansaekhwa shared cannot be seen in mere formalistic terms but in the desire to root painting in the consciousness of change and transformation witnessed in the post–Korean War era.

1 Lee Kyung Sung, "Director's Preface," in *Working with Nature: Traditional Thought in Contemporary Art from Korea* exh. cat., (Liverpool: Tate Gallery Liverpool, 1992), 8. This was the catalogue for an exhibition co-organized by Tate Gallery Liverpool and the National Museum of Modern and Contemporary Art, Seoul.

2 Lewis Biggs, "Working with Nature: Selector's Introduction," in *Working with Nature*, 8–13.

3 Lee Yil, "On 'Working with Nature,'" in *Working with Nature*, 14–16.

4 Ha was professor in the College of Fine Arts at Hongik University from 1967 to 2001 and served as dean from 1990 to 1994. From 1962 to 1966, he worked as a lecturer there. He is currently emeritus professor.

5 Kyung An, "A Spirit of Experimentation: Ha Chong Hyun before Dansaekhwa, 1967–74," in *Ha Chong Hyun* (Seoul/New York: Kukje Gallery/Gregory R. Miller & Co., 2017), 22.

6 Taro Nettleton, "Interview: Ha Chong-Hyun—Convergence of Mass," *Bijutsu Techo*, Spring 2016, 36–43.

7 Transcript from Dansaekhwa Symposium, hosted by Kukje Gallery, Seoul, South Korea, January 23–24, 2015, collateral event of the 56th International Art Exhibition, in Yongwoo Lee, ed., *Dansaekhwa* exh. cat. (Seoul: Kukje Gallery, 2015), 274–87.

8 Transcript from Dansaekhwa Symposium, in *Dansaekhwa* exh. cat., 274–87.

9 Yoon Jin-Sup "The World of Dansaekhwa: Spirit, Tactility, and Performance," in *The Art of Dansaekhwa* (Seoul: Kukje Gallery, 2014), 19–25.

Installation view of *Dansaekhwa*, Palazzo Contarini-Polignac, Venice, Italy, 2015.

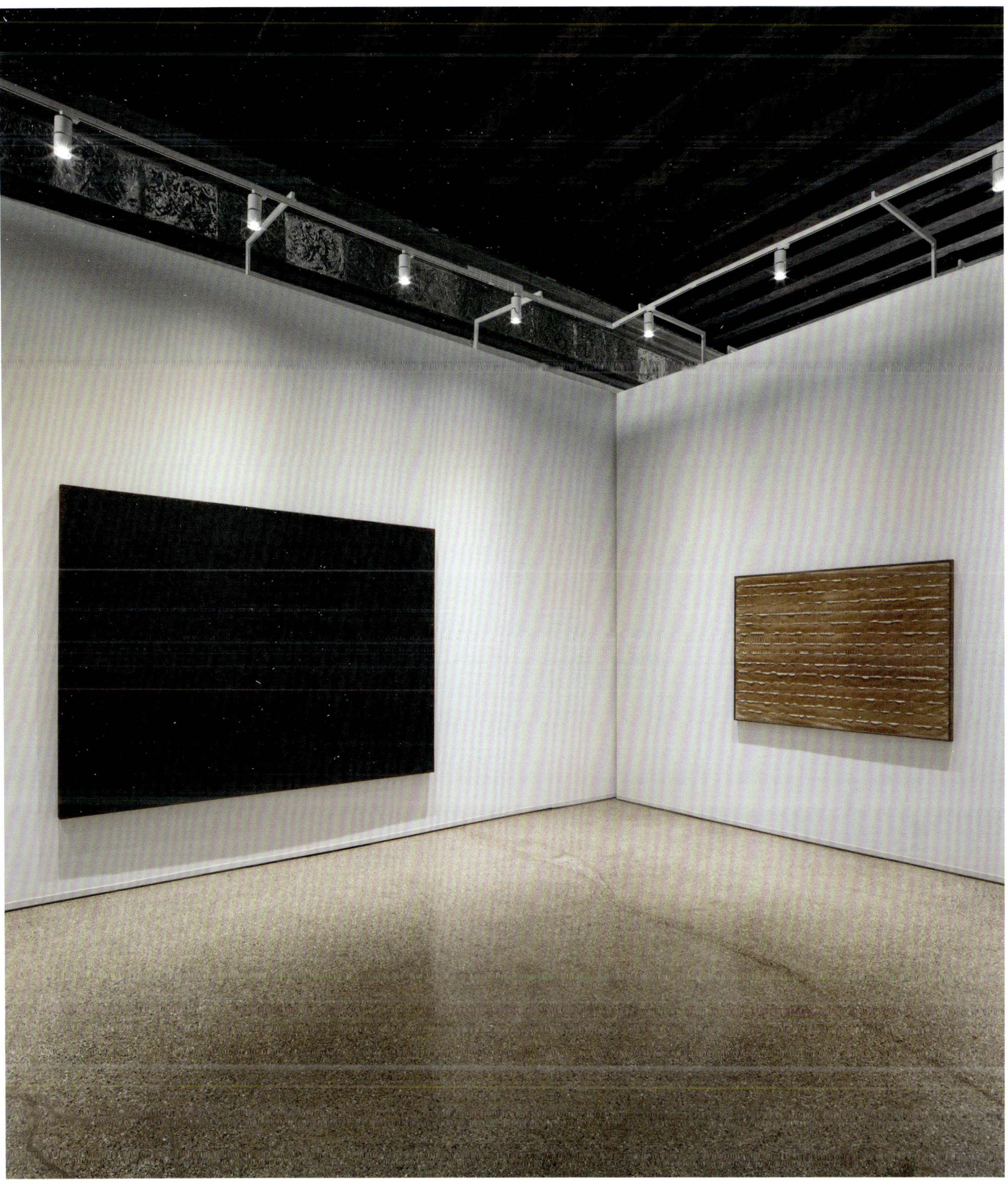

HA CHONG-HYUN'S EARLY WORK AND THE EXPERIMENTAL AG GROUP

YEON SHIM CHUNG

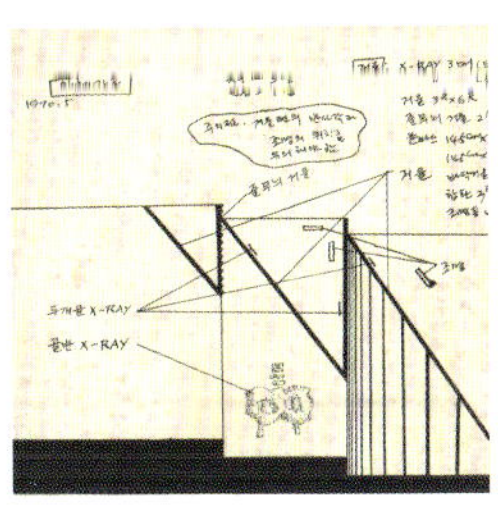

FIG 6

Ha Chong-Hyun's *Amulette V* and *Amulette VI*, exhibited at the fourth Biennale de Paris in 1965, render the collective unconsciousness of wounds and ritual, as the titles of the works suggest.[1] Leading Korean art critic and Ha's close friend Lee Yil noted that the Informel-style work has "traces of tragic emotion."[2] Lee was critical of the vestiges of Informel that Korean artists showed at the biennale that year, claiming that there was a discrepancy between their sensibility and their methods of expression. Because Lee lived in Paris from 1957 to 1966, he was conscious of the gazes with which French critics looked at Korean modern art; as he observed, "Europeans try to search for 'Oriental' and 'traditional' elements before they look at actual works of art from Korea."[3]

The 1950s in Korea brought about Informel; beginning in 1957, paintings recalled the psychological trauma and vestiges of the Korea War. The thick *matière*—dominated by dark, gloomy colors—reflects the era's existential feeling and the deep sorrow of the war's aftermath. The lacerations of conflict and the traces of them that persisted long after liberation became dominant characteristics of the postwar generation. However, this somber palette underwent a transformation in the mid-1960s, incited by the April 19 generation, whose social demonstrations forced President Syngman Rhee to resign over allegations of election rigging. Korean art of the 1960s epitomized an experimental, artistic approach toward new reforms, political changes, and economic expectations, despite omnipresent social turmoil. The avant-garde artists of this era resisted the annual nationally-sponsored art exhibition and rejected its corrupt jury systems and conservative thematic choices, characterized by landscapes without any realistic portrayals of people in such genres as painting, sculpture, crafts, and so on.

Young artists in their twenties and thirties, including the artists of Informel, experimented with new mediums and innovative techniques as an artistic imperative, criticizing the country's art administration in the absence of a national museum of art in Korea. Indeed, at the time art was exhibited at the National Information Center, whose mission was to promote Korean industrial and commercial products for export. Beginning in the 1960s, a strong aspiration for change and an affinity with causes of resistance and innovation, along with the transformation that followed the massive urbanization of Seoul, had a profound impact upon both art and society.[4]

AG EXHIBITIONS AND HA CHONG HYUN'S WORK

As Lee Yil noted in evoking the new sensitivities of the era, avant-garde art was no longer an art of rebellion or protest, but one of participation.[5] According to Lee, this radicality is predicated on entering one's most immediate present or reality, and breaking out of a solipsistic introspectiveness. To be precise, Lee's use of "participation" stems from French Nouveau Réalisme, but he found its meanings in the young Korean avant-garde's experimental art in direct response to their own environment and social situations. In the eyes of young critic Lee, who had just returned to Seoul from Paris, these AG artists, including Ha Chong-Hyun, participated in urban civilization. It was thus a new reality that young experimentalists captured.

AG (Avant-Garde Association), established in the subversive anti-art spirit of 1969, published an eponymous art journal, curated four exhibitions, and organized the Seoul Biennale in 1974, before dissolving in 1975. The mission of the *AG* journal, as stated in its frontispiece, was to "contribute to the progress of Korean art and culture by exploring and creating a new plastic order in the visionless Korean art worlds on the basis of strong consciousness toward avant-garde art."[6] It was in this journal that Lee Ufan's "Introduction to the Phenomenology of Encounter: To Prepare for a New Art Theory" was published,[7] and the phenomenological dialogue of object and its surrounding or its site influenced young artists. In particular, the aesthetic emphasis on participation was applied to the editorial direction of the essays included in the association's journal and exhibitions. The *AG* journal was helmed by the leading critics of the times; Lee Yil, Oh Kwang-Su, Kim In-Hwan, Ha Chong-Hyun, and other participants in the exhibitions dealt in their work with this new emphasis on material realism, a changing yet oppressive society and urban culture, and the new art of the era as "environmental art."[8] All the participants supported the singular, individual results of these new artworks, rejecting orthodox artistic forms and embracing an avant-garde attitude and experimentalism that embodied what Lee Yil described as "new methods."

Apart from the journal, AG also published catalogues to accompany its exhibitions, and often the artists designed the catalogues themselves, as they considered the medium of print a new art production and technology.[9] In particular, the catalogue of the second AG exhibition, which took place in 1971 at the newly-founded National Museum of Modern and Contemporary Art at Gyeongbokgung Palace, was published after the temporary installations were already in place, stressing the site-specificity of the works. With the exception of a few two-dimensional works, reproductions in the catalogues attest to their original sites and the context of the exhibition.

Ha Chong-Hyun was one of the leading artists of AG, and one of the few who participated in all four AG exhibitions and the 1974 Seoul Biennale. In the first AG exhibition, *The Dynamics of Expansion and Reduction*, Ha installed a temporary art piece called *Work* (fig. 6).[10] This installation required three carpenters and an art specialist to set up and consisted of three x-ray images showing a skull and pelvis, a plain mirror, a striped mirror, canvas, plywood, lighting, and other materials. In an interview, the artist said that the mirror and x-rays were chosen to embody the new material realism associated with civilization, in order to reconsider or rethink what had been lost in the rapid economic progress and modernization in contemporary Korea.[11] The installation was meant to evoke an environment at once newly built and wholly destroyed—an environment of rapid modernization.

As Lee wrote in his essay for the exhibition, spectators "experience, behave, and perceive" inside of the work.[12] In his essay "Dynamics of Expansion and Reduction," he explains that the artworks come "from the most fundamental of forms to events that happen in the course of everyday life, from the most direct and immediate experiences to objects that are the materialization of a concept," situating art "not in its

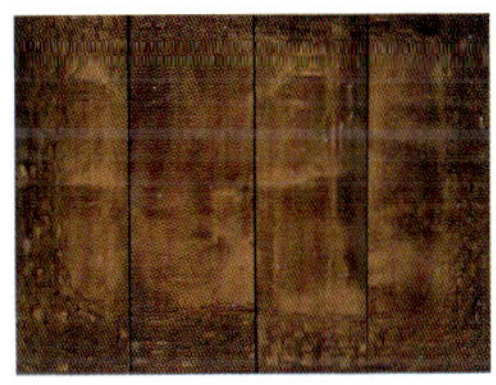

FIG 7

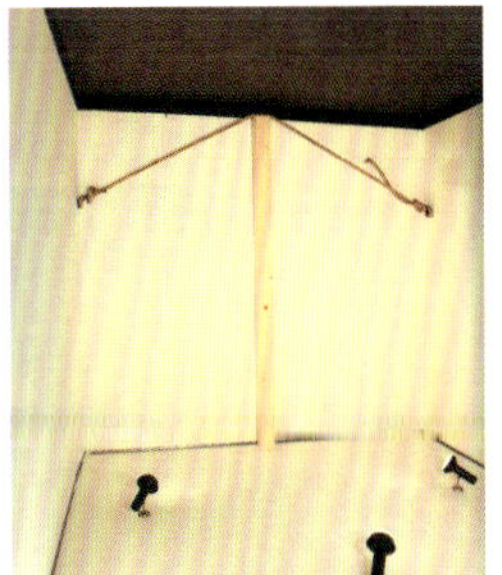

FIG 8

being 'art' but in its being a confirmation of life. . . . A nameless object, because of its anonymity, opens onto a colorful existence and leads us toward the adventure of new perception." This "anti-art" now "returns to its zero degree." This kind of new possibility of art does not address forms or shapes but exists in the "expansion of reality" and "the field of experiences," furthering "a trigger of spiritual adventure."[13]

Art as a field of experience and environment corresponds to the "environmentalization of space art" that Lee discussed in his essay "Experimental Avant-Garde," published in *AG*. Related to the "expansion" of the first AG exhibition itself, Lee's reformulation of expansion draws connections to the "environment, our urban environment, nature environment, that is an extension of living space."[14] Spectators find themselves "caught in the environment," defining the new spectatorship in the correspondence of art and life.[15] Similarly, in "From Space Dynamics to Time Dynamics: The Case of Nicolas Schöffer," Lee discusses multi-sensory art in the use of technology, merging art, architecture, and urban planning, and explaining that "art can become an industrial object, industrial thing" that does not exist as a complete, finished artwork.[16] This attitude was pervasive among the participants in the AG exhibitions, where artists employed found materials, such as newspapers, stones, earth, mirrors, cloth, cement, and so on.

AG exhibitions also addressed the subject of dematerialized status, using wind or ice. In this way they explored the structural and anti-structural object within the locality of its site and exposed the temporality and materiality of the object, to the extent that it degrades into a thing (an operation similar to Arte Povera). Social and environmental changes such as modernization, industrialization, urbanization, and the construction of "commune" houses (namely, Korean-style apartments under the five-year economic development plan of the third Republic of Korea) had a substantial impact on these avant-garde artists. For example, AG artist Choi Myoung-Young exhibited *Transformation 70-B* using concrete drains and clothes to illustrate the changing urban architecture culture in Seoul.[17]

Ha Chong-Hyun has argued, "The times in which tableau existed as the only form have passed in favor of the *gesamtkunstwerk* of painting, sculpture, architecture, design, and so on."[18] Earlier, in 1967, Ha produced the remarkable work *White Paper on Urban Planning* (see p. 53). Its geometric forms and colors formulated a direct response to the society and environment of the time. The title derives from an ongoing conversation between the artist and Lee Yil (several versions of *White Paper* exist, dated from 1967 to 1969 or 1970). The year 1967 was a time when avant-garde experimentalists sought a new geometric abstraction at the intersection of society and the environment; likewise, it was a time of pivotal change for Ha. The artist dramatically renounced Informel and, just as the Constructivists had defined a new city and humanity, he discarded expressionist traces and the epic wounds of war as he took up geometric patterns.[19] Having described Ha's Informel-style work as a "shriveled, dried squid," Lee praised Ha's works of 1967 as "a remarkable transformation." Indeed, *White Paper* won the art award of the leading architectural magazine *Space*.[20]

It is important to note that *Space* was the first Korean architectural magazine, founded by the prominent Korean modernist architect Kim Swoo-Geun in late 1966. The first issue (November 1966) included a special feature titled "Seoul Urban Basic Planning," and another feature titled "Seoul, 1967" appeared in the September 1967 issue. With the close relationship between the avant-garde artists and the architect at the top of the magazine's masthead, themes of Seoul's urban planning and the metropolis as a city structure stimulated discussion of the new city taking form and the place of avant-garde art.[21] In the pages of *Space,* Sung Chan-Kyung described the Seoul of 1970 as "a cannibalistic struggle between the past and the present" and wrote that the city was transforming from "traditional *dancheong* to veneer plywood . . . wood to cement, spadework to bulldozer, sugarcane to iron frame, individuality to group, Seoul 1970 to explosion."[22]

In this milieu, Ha's *Composition*, created in 1967, entered into Lee Yil's discourse of "urban civilization and environmentalization of life,"[23] situating Ha's work beyond his canvas's frame. Thus, avant-garde art became linked with expanded social construction and geometric composition, in a style reminiscent of that of the Russian Constructivists. Another work, *Naissance* (1967),[24] is filled with abstract and geometric patterns, seed-like shapes that repeat, and colors and forms that lack "individuality,"[25] and that reflect the social tone of the era.

At the second and third AG exhibitions, Ha Chong-Hyun installed more socially engaged pieces, addressing the oppressed social situation itself. For the 1971 exhibition, the artist created an installation (fig. 5) in which he juxtaposed daily newspapers with blank, unprinted white paper. Korean news media in the 1970s was highly censored, and the work revealed how the circulation of information was used to control and oppress Korean society at the time. Like the temporary *Work* that Ha showed in the first AG exhibition, *Counter-Phase* was a temporary, site-specific installation; spectators were invited to experience rigid society, suppression, and censorship within the limits of the exhibition space. Censored newspapers and unprinted white paper were paired to signify the political condition of the times and the condition of the thing, respectively. Ha, who was then teaching studio art at Hongik University, also witnessed student demonstrations against the government, and this work was a reflection of his anguish over the generational defiance.

In line with *Counter-Phase*, for the third AG exhibition Ha created *Untitled 72*, featuring tangled coils of wire repetitively and compulsively accumulated on the surface of the canvas.[26] He twisted barbed wire and crossed it horizontally to create a strong psychological tension of line and surface. Around the same time, Ha also created an untitled series in which he bound the front or back of each panel with wire. Philippe Dagen, commenting on these works, found unavoidable allusions to "camps, prisons, raids, martial law, sentencing, and war," and "saturation, containment, silence, oppression, abstinence, contraction." Dagen argued that "the length of wire encloses and pierces the canvas as if imprisoning and harming a body."[27] All the colors and geometric forms or images that Ha employed in his early paintings in the mid- to late 1960s are gone in these works, leaving only rigidly arranged grid structures with loose

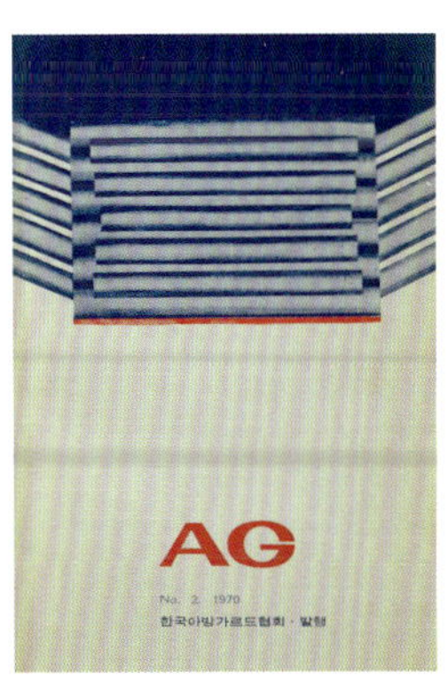

FIG 9

or coiled barbed wire and springs. The austere surfaces, with wires that tighten the vertical and the horizontal planes, constrict the viewer's gaze, leading them to focus on the pain or tension of the rectangular grids themselves, which stress the object's conditions of materiality. Such a visceral sensation of viewership is comparable to Lee Ufan's *Structure*, made by cutting wood with a planer (fig. 7).[28]

Ha's *Relation* (1971), *Relation 72-1* (1972, fig. 4), *Work 72-7* (fig. 11), and other series from 1972 (many of which were shown at his solo exhibition at the Myung-Dong gallery in Seoul) also capture the conditions and tension of the object and its surroundings.[29] In particular, in *Relation 72-1* the taut rope causes a tension that literally seems about to explode. Lee Yil characterized his focus on presentation of "matter" (i.e., material) and "materialized space"—a focus that then continued in the *Conjunction* series—as stemming from this period.[30]

Political systems in Korea did not modernize in parallel with urbanization. The remnants of the Cold War remained, creating extreme tension between the two Koreas. The unstable politics were intensified in 1972 by the Yushin Constitution under the fourth republic of president Park Chung-Hee; the constitution cemented Park's dictatorship and abuse of human rights, going so far as to limit citizens' freedom to choose individual styles and tastes. It formed a striking contrast to Ha's *White Paper on Urban Planning*, and the restraint of Ha's handmade barbed wires and springs signaled the oppressed political situation of the 1970s.

HA CHONG-HYUN'S ESSAY PUBLISHED IN *AG*

To understand Ha's experimental early works, one needs to study his early writings, which reflect his aesthetic attitudes and ideas. In particular, "Entering the Year of 1970 in Korean Art," published in *AG* in 1970 (fig. 9), contains several important aspects of his views as an artist: the lack of art/artist support systems on the institutional level, harsh criticism of the national exhibition systems, the expansion of international art exhibitions to include young artists, and a more fierce, experimental spirit in strong support of non-materiality in art and technology (a reflection of changing sociopolitical and economic contexts in contemporary Korea).

Ha begins by explicating the changes of his time as follows:

> The year of 1970 is filled with many surprising events. A highly advanced scientific cultivation led humanity to land on the moon, and historical steps were taken toward unveiling the mystery of 4.5 billion years. Likewise, the art world experienced seemingly remarkable aesthetic changes that are comparable to the art historical changes achieved over the past centuries. . . . However, what about the activities of the 1960s in the art world in Korea? . . . It is belated yet fortunate to see the opening of the National Museum of Modern and Contemporary Art (in 1969) and that the government was committed to reforming the national exhibition systems as well as international exhibition support.[31]

After this criticism, he urges the government to encourage Korean artists to participate in international exhibitions, as they did with the Paris biennale in the 1960s. He notes the separation of non-objective abstract art (such as performance) from objective genres of paintings in state-sponsored art exhibitions. Although Informel art was an "avant-garde" movement in its time in the late 1950s, over the 1960s, according to Ha, the Informel-dominated national art exhibitions became an "abstract academicism, neglecting the emergence of new values or concepts."[32]

Ha goes on to write that the emergence of Informel art in Korea was an "inevitable opportunity" to rise up from the ruins of the Korean War (1950–1953) but that there was "in the background a loss of trust toward the established order and values, and the social crisis of consciousness."[33] In the decade after Informel emerged in 1957, its aesthetics became widespread enough to form the artistic mainstream. However, with the influx of economic changes and urban cultures, as well as social transformation, the art of the past undertook new, urban transformations, making way for an art of the city. Ha notes these characteristics of contemporary art in the late 1960s:

> The visible characteristics that distinguish the art of the contemporary from the past are those of urban art. Urban art is tied to mass production and information, a rational and cold atmosphere, the scales and geometric forms that are apparent in modern urban architecture—factory chimneys, gas tanks, and so on. The social form related to monuments in the absence of artists became major factors in overthrowing the artistic concepts that used to exist in the world.[34]

Ha does not provide a comprehensive list of artists' names, but he traces the avant-garde spirit of the 1960s to the Origin group established in 1963, mentioning artists Suh Seung-Won, Choi Myoung-Young and Lee Seung-Jio in defense of cold geometric forms. The new spirit of object-oriented experimental art, such as the employment of light as a material, and dematerialized happenings, continued to diversify artistic mediums and concepts. These new experiments in postwar Korean art were considered "international contemporaneity" or "international simultaneity" among young avant-gardists.[35] To spread awareness of contemporaneity, *AG* published several articles on international contemporary art, including one on *concetto spaziale* by Lucio Fontana (1899–1968), and a translation of David Shirey's article on impossible art (first published in *Art in America*'s May/June 1969 issue), which discussed Dennis Oppenheim's earth art, Joseph Kosuth's conceptual art, and Archigram.

It is notable that a sense of "international contemporaneity" was discursively grounded in artists' readings of foreign magazines, critical writings, and books, rather than direct exposure via travel to Europe or the United States. Based on the changes in the 1960s, Ha further explains a new attitude in the arts:

> As means of communication develop and grow faster, the time needed for art movements that take place in major cities of the world to be signaled over a great distance shrinks, and international simultaneity

can be found in the Korean art world, in terms of the expressions of synesthetic sympathy of artists living in the contemporary era. The times in which tableau existed as the only form have passed in favor of the *gesamtkunstwerk* of painting, sculpture, architecture, design, and so on. The artist's strong fever, free from the gravity of the earth as well as all the concerns of the 1970s in anticipation of space development, will find a new possibility in the name of space aesthetics. Also, elemental materials such as air, water, earth, and fire will cross the transformation of our sensitivities and perceptions with technology in unexpected ways, all of which will lead us to recover the original "nature" in the end.[36]

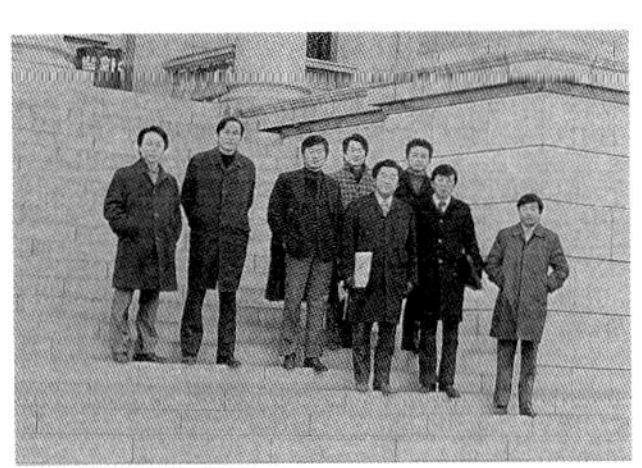

FIG 10

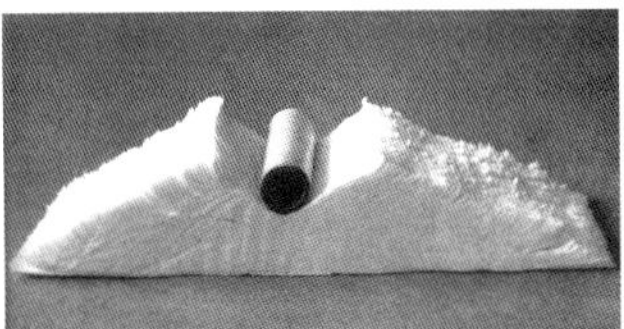

FIG 11

The last sentence presages the years that followed, which were characterized by global art's expansion of artistic media, as well as Ha's own return to the pictorial surfaces of the *Conjunction* series.

AG AND THE 1974 SEOUL BIENNALE

The final AG exhibition took place in 1975, but only four artists—Ha Chong-Hyun, Lee Kun-Yong, Shin Hak-Chul, and Kim Han—participated, and AG's collective identity dissolved. A more extensive exhibition curated by AG was the 1974 Seoul Biennale[37] (fig. 10), motivated by the desire to organize an international biennale and partly inspired by the Biennale de Paris. Launched in 1959, the Paris biennale began including Korean artists in 1961, when Paris based critic Lee Yil and Park Seo-Bo arranged to exhibit work by Kim Tschang-Yeul, Kim Byung-Ki, Cho Yong-Ik, and others.

The 1974 Seoul Biennale catalogue indicates that the president of the biennale was Ha Chong-Hyun, and Lee Yil was the commissioner. This exhibition was open to other experimental artists, and it was characterized by temporary installations and concept-based projects. Lee defined it as "the search for a method" in the spirit of resistance and subjective criticism that paid attention to the movement of the young generation. He noted that "although each artist faces a different problem, the exhibition was focused on their search for a method and his/her own presentation of concept."[38] Lee's concepts of "method" and "the ethic of resistance" and "international contemporaneity" were important to his argument of "subjective critical spirit,"[39] but the experiments and their singularities did not develop as Lee or Ha expected.

However, it should be noted that, in the twenty years since the advent of modern art in Korea after 1953 (the end of the Korean War), there had never been a moment when both experimental and fiercely anti-art activities and exhibitions were considered more profoundly important. By establishing the Seoul Biennale, these young artists and critics aspired to interact with other artists around the globe, but without any support from professional systems and art institutions, the biennale started and ended with that first edition. At that time, the Korean art scene was dominated by the national art exhibitions, yet Ha Chong-Hyun and other experimental artists rejected the state-sponsored shows, preferring independent, anti-institutionalized, temporary exhibitions or projects.

The critical direction of the *AG* journal and the artists' works did not always coincide, but with an avant-garde spirit, Ha and his contemporaries explored the new context of art and artistic method as much as they explored new mediums.

Although the national art exhibitions and the newly founded National Museum of Modern and Contemporary Art in Korea categorized art by traditional genre, AG artists attempted hybridity, intersecting and transcending different artistic mediums. By doing so, Ha and his fellow AG artists produced a new trajectory of art with the idea of Lee's "subjective criticism" and "methods," whereby art creates a new environment in the expanded field of everyday life. This was a new and strange artistic concept in Korea in the 1970s. Ha Chong-Hyun's encounter with the materiality of the object, the social environment, and the body were embedded in the dynamics and diversity of experimental arts raised by the different groups of artists within AG, in pursuit of plural voices in their singularities. Ha advocated strongly for the importance of the body and physical collision with painting vis-à-vis non-painting, an attitude that would reappear in his oeuvre across the decades that followed.

1 *Quatrième Biennale de Paris* exh. cat. (Paris: Biennale de Paris, 1965), 45–46. The commissioner was Park Seo-Bo and Lee Yil wrote an essay on Korean artists for the biennale.

2 Lee Yil, "Notes on the Fourth Paris Biennale (1965)," in *Lee Yil Anthology*, ed. Yeon Shim Chung et. al. (Seoul: Mijinsa, 2015), 297, 305. This experience in Paris began his quest for and questions about Korean tradition.

3 Lee, "Notes on the Fourth Paris Biennale," 297.

4 Old housing was demolished to build new apartment complexes, while narrow roads were removed to make standardized street systems to accommodate the new social demands of urban dwellers.

5 Lee, *Lee Yil Anthology*, 43, 47, 125. Lee Yil's concept of "an art of participation" was influenced and inspired by Pierre Restany.

6 This motto appeared on the front pages of the *AG* journals. AG published four issues: June 1969, March 1970, May 1970, and November 1971.

7 See *AG* 4 (November 1971): 5–14.

8 For environmentalization, Lee Yil quotes Frederick Kiesler and Kynaston McShine's preface to a catalogue for the exhibition *Primary Structures: Younger American and British Sculptors*, held at the Jewish Museum, New York, in 1966. See Lee Yil, "Notes on Avant-Garde Art," *AG* 1 (June 1969): 2–10; reprinted in *Lee Yil Anthology*, 123–29.

9 Park Suk-Won, interview with the author, July 29, 2021 and January 6, 2022.

10 The first AG exhibition took place at the National Information Center (May 1–17, 1970), and its catalogue was included in the journal *AG* 3 (May 1970): 4–16. Twelve AG members participated in this exhibition: Kim Kulim, Kim Tchah-Sup, Kim Han, Kim Chong-Bae, Park Suk-Won, Suh Seung-Won, Shin Hak-Chul, Lee Seung-Jio, Choi Myoung-Young, Shim Moon-Seup, Lee Seung Taek, and Ha Chong-Hyun.

11 Ha Chong-Hyun, interview with the author, January 12, 2022.

12 Lee, *Lee Yil Anthology*, 393: see also Kim Bok-Young, "The Phenomenology of Thing and Body," *Space*, May 1984, 100–106. Lee recalls Maurice Merleau-Ponty's concept of making things present themselves through the body.

13 Lee Yil, "Dynamics of Expansion and Reduction (1970)," in *Lee Yil: Selected Writings on Korean Contemporary Art*, ed. Yeon Shim Chung and Jean Marc Poinsot (Paris: Les Presses du reel, 2018), 20.

14 Lee Yil, "Experimental Avant-Garde," *AG* 1 (June 1969): 2–10; and Lee Yil, "Aesthetic Endeavors: Object Art" in *Lee Yil Anthology*, 157–61.

15 Lee, "Experimental Avant-Garde"; and Lee, "Aesthetic Endeavors: Object Art."

16 Lee Yil, "From Space Dynamics to Time Dynamics: The Case of Nicolas Schöffer," *AG* 2 (March 1970): 12–17. This statement might remind one of Michael Fried's concept of "objecthood," but there is no clear evidence that Lee read Fried's "Art and Objecthood," published in *Artforum* 5 (June 1967): 12–23.

17 For the first AG exhibition in 1970, Kim Kulim installed *From Phenomenon to Trace*, a site project that experimented with ice and the condition of temporality, which the catalogue reproduced under the title *Traces*.

18 Ha Chong-Hyun, "Entering the Year of 1970 in Korean Art," *AG* 2 (March 1970): 2–3.

19 Lee Yil, "Ha Chong-Hyun: Non-Painterly Painting (1984)," in *Lee Yil: Selected Writings on Korean Contemporary Art*, 159.

20 See Ha Chong-Hyun's essay on this award in *Space*, September 1975, 60–62.

21 See "Seoul Urban Basic Planning," *Space*, November 1966, 8–16; and "Seoul, 1967," *Space*, September 1967, 5–27.

22 Sung Chan-Kyung, "Surrounding Boundaries and Worlds, Seoul, 1970," *Space*, February 1970, 26.

23 Lee Yil, "Protest and Participation in Art (1965)," in *Lee Yil Anthology*, 43.

24 There are three versions of this work: *Naissance–A* is housed at the National Museum of Modern and Contemporary Art in Korea, *Naissance–C* is at the Hongik University Museum, and *Naissance–B* was auctioned in 2020 in Korea.

25 You Jae-Gil, "Korean Geometric Abstraction and Op-art," in *The 40 Years of Korean Abstract Art* (Seoul: Jaewon, 1997), 86–87.

26 Such artists as Kim Kulim, Kim Dong-Gyu, Kim Han, Park Suk-Won, Park Chong-Bae, Suh Seung-Won, Shin Hak-Chul, Shim Moon-Seup, Lee Kang-So, Lee Kun-Yong, Lee Seung-Jio, and Choi Myoung-Young participated in the third AG exhibition. Looking at the exhibition photos in Park Suk-Won's collection, one can see that Lee Kun-Yong installed *Relation*, which differs from the image reproduced in the catalogue (of 1972). The indeterminate relation between the object and the site where it is placed shows that the avant-gardists in AG were influenced by Lee Ufan's Mono-ha.

27 Philippe Dagen, "Ha Chong Hyun, Concern and Silence," in *Ha Chong-Hyun* (Seoul: Gana Art Center, 2008), 19, 21.

28 See Lee Ufan, "The Identity of Object Aesthetics and the Search for It," *Hongik Misul* 1 (1972): 86–96.

29 "Ha Chong-Hyun's First Solo Exhibition," *Chosun Ilbo*, June 8, 1974.

30 Lee Yil, "On Ha Chong-Hyun's Exhibition," in *Ha Chong-Hyun* exh. cat. (Seoul: Myung-Dong Gallery, 1974), n.p.; reprinted in *Lee Yil Anthology*, 32.

31 Ha Chong-Hyun, "Entering the Year of 1970 in Korean Art," *AG* 2 (March 1970): 2.

32 Ha, "Entering the Year of 1970 in Korean Art," 2.

33 Ha, "Entering the Year of 1970 in Korean Art," 3.

34 Ha, "Entering the Year of 1970 in Korean Art," 3.

35 Ha, "Entering the Year of 1970 in Korean Art," 3.

36 Ha, "Entering the Year of 1970 in Korean Art," 2–3.

37 It is notable that in 1974 experimental artists also organized the second *Indépendant* exhibition at the National Museum of Modern and Contemporary Art in Seoul.

38 Lee Yil, "For a New Perspective," in *The First Seoul Biennale* exh. cat. (Seoul: Seoul Biennale, 1974), n.p.; reprinted in *Lee Yil Anthology,* 385–86.

39 Lee Yil, "The Crossroads of Environment and Expectation: Looking Back at the Year of 1974," *Space*, January 1975, 12–13; reprinted in *Lee Yil Anthology*, 395–97. Lee Yil writes, "Today's outsiders will be tomorrow's protagonists; I want to share such faith and pride with the young generation of artists." The critic notes that the young artists who led AG were a generational driving force behind exhibitions, including the Seoul Biennale.

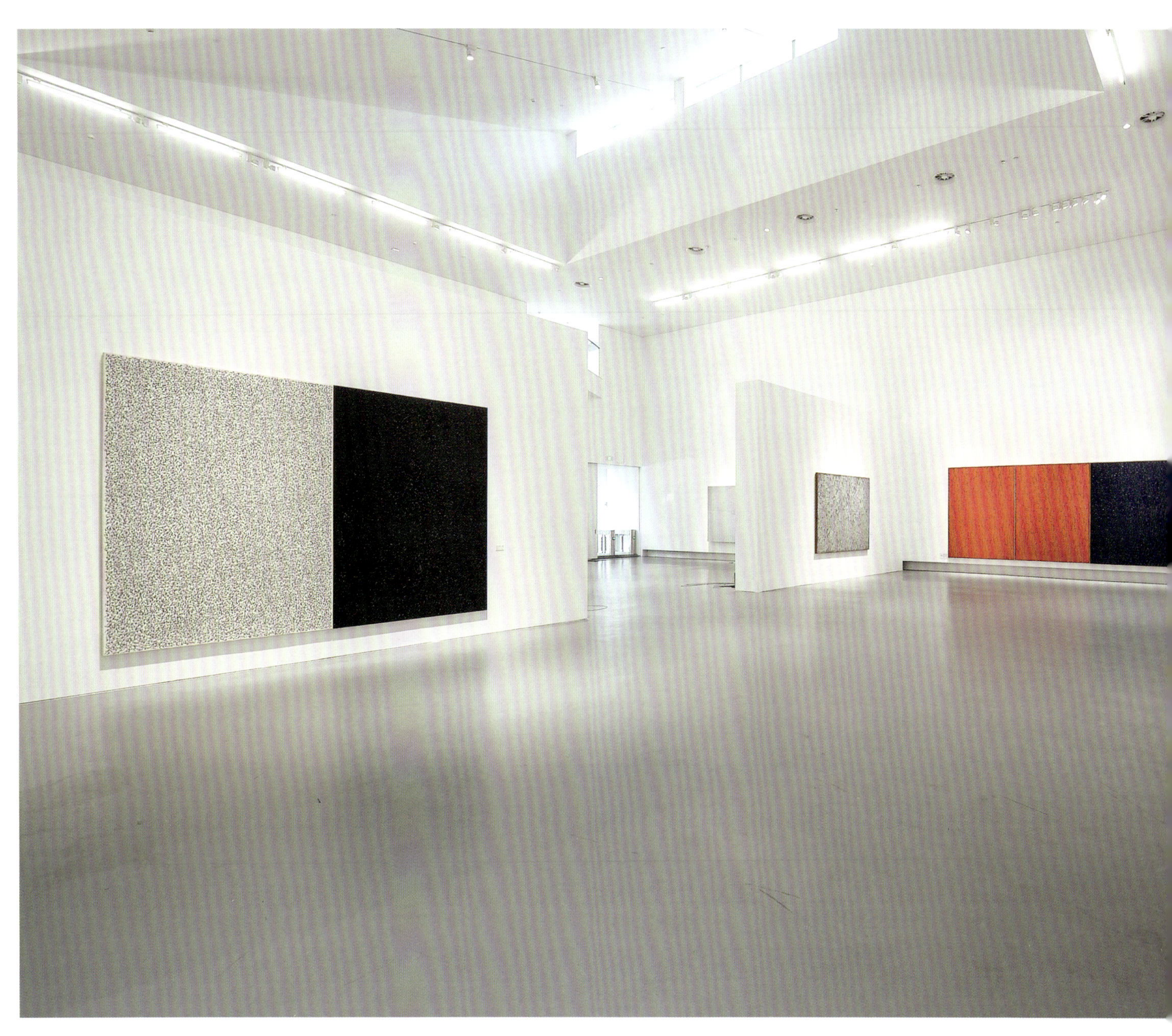

Installation view of *Korean Abstract Art: Kim Whanki and Dansaekhwa*, Powerlong Museum, Shanghai, China. November 8, 2018–March 2, 2019.

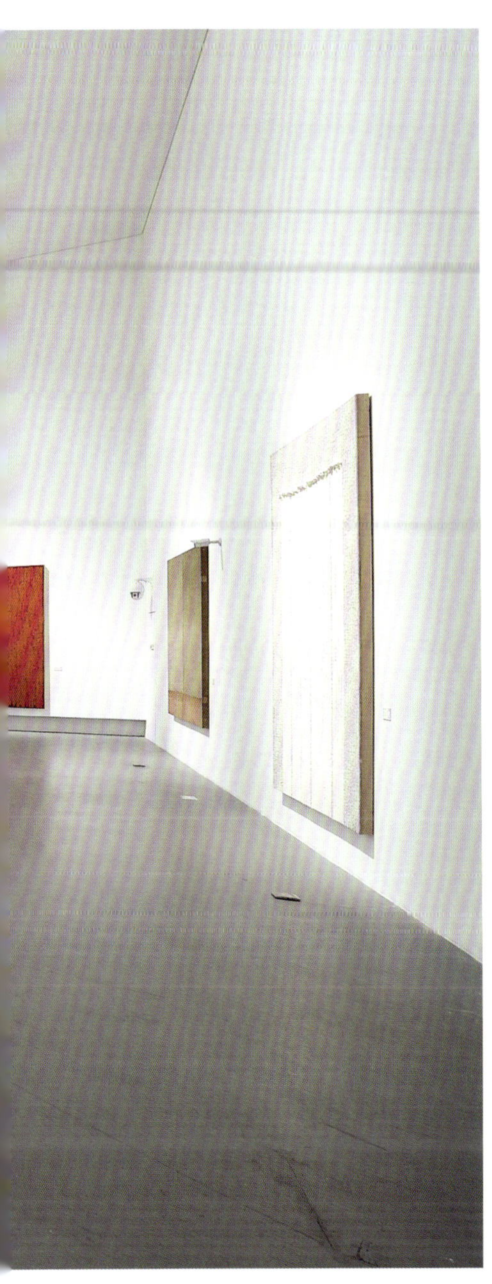

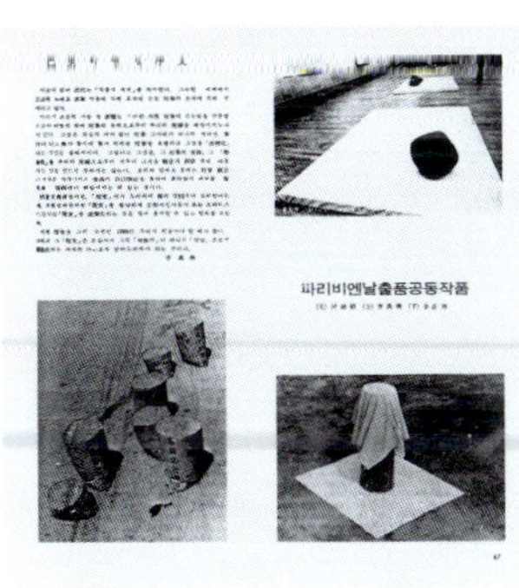

2nd Biennale de Paris, 1961, Musée d'art Moderne de la Ville de Paris.

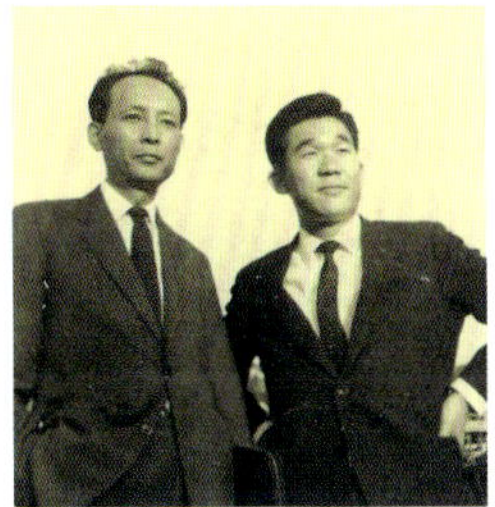

Ha Chong-Hyun (right) with art critic Lee Yil, 1960s, Seoul, Korea.

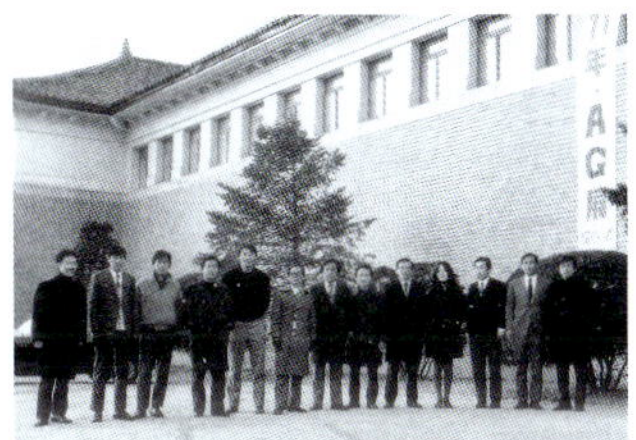

Ha Chong-Hyun (fourth from left) and other artists who participated in the AG exhibition, 1971.

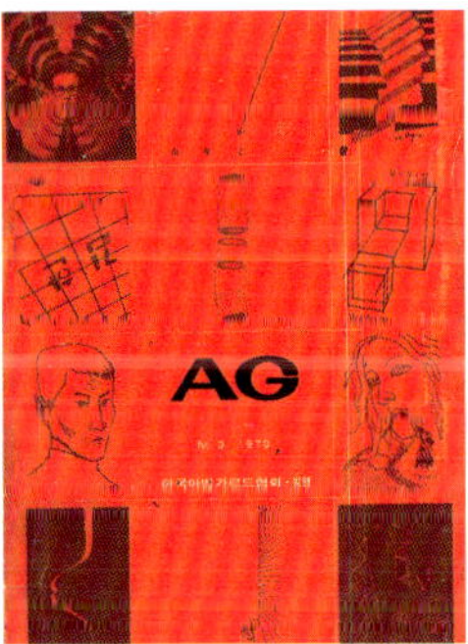

Cover of journal *AG* 3, May 1970.

1935 Ha Chong-Hyun is born in Sancheong, Korea.

1945 Thirty-five years of Japanese colonial rule end in Korea.

1950 The Korean War begins.

1956 Park Seo-Bo, Kim Young-Hwan, Kim Choong-Sun, and Moon Woo-Sik organize *Four Artists' Show* at Dongbang Cultural Center, Seoul, Korea and establish the anti-national exhibition movement.

Art Critic Ki Yong-Ju introduces the word "Informel" into Korean art criticism.

1957 The Korean Contemporary Artists Association is established.

1959 Major art movements from Europe, the United States, and Japan, such as Abstract Expressionism and Art Informel, begin to influence a new generation of Korean artists.

Ha Chong-Hyun graduates from Hongik University and begins producing abstract works categorized under the rubric of "Korean Informel."

1961 Korea participates in the 2nd Biennale de Paris in France.

1965 Korea and Japan restore diplomatic relations.

Ha Chong-Hyun and Lee Ufan participate in the 4th Biennale de Paris.

1967 Ha Chong-Hyun participates in the 9th São Paulo Bienal, Brazil, as part of the Korean delegation.

Ha Chong-Hyun shows a work from the *White Paper on Urban Planning* series at the 11th Invitational Exhibition of Contemporary Artists, Seoul, Korea.

1968 The AG (Avant Garde Association) is established in Seoul by artists associated with Hongik University, including Ha Chong-Hyun, followed by publication of the inaugural issue of *AG* journal the following year.

1969–1974 Ha Chong-Hyun serves as chairman of AG.

1970 Korean avant-garde groups, including the Fourth Group and the Space & Time (S.T.) Group, are formed.

Ha Chong-Hyun publishes "Entering the Year of 1970 in Korean Art" in the second issue of the journal *AG*.

1971 Ha Chong-Hyun participates in the seminal second AG exhibition, *Reality and Realization*, at the National Museum of Modern and Contemporary Art, Seoul, Korea.

1972 General Park Chung-Hee declares martial law and amends the existing constitution into a new document titled the Yushin Constitution.

1972 Korea participates in the 2nd Biennale de Paris.

Ha Chong-Hyun's *Work 72-3 (B)* is included in the third AG exhibition at the National Museum of Modern and Contemporary Art, Seoul.

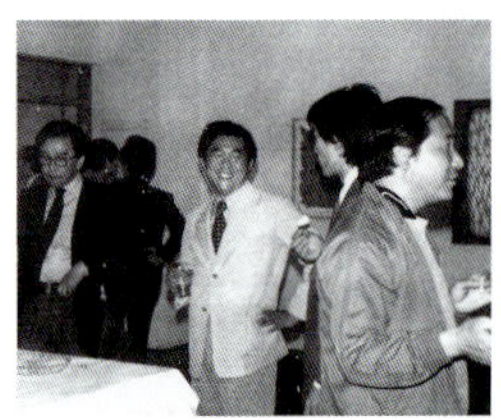

Ha Chong-Hyun, early 1970s.

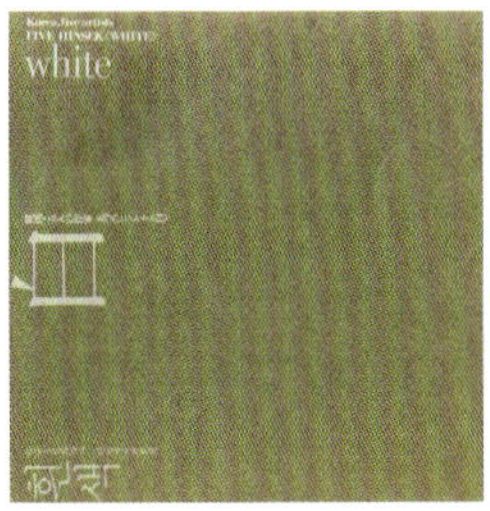

Five Korean Artists, Five Kinds of White, 1975, Tokyo Gallery.

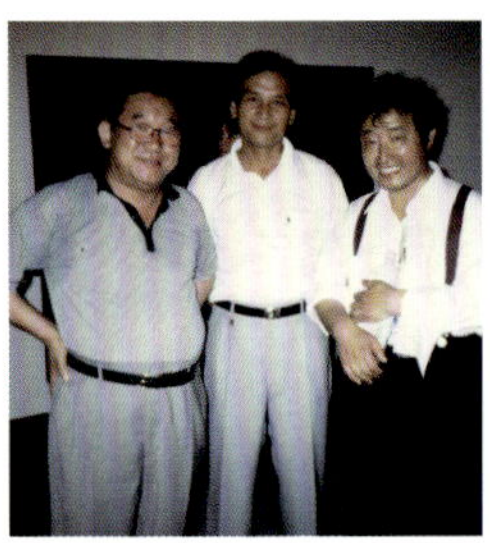

From left to right: Ha Chong-Hyun, Suh Seung-Won, Nam June Paik.

1972 Ha Chong-Hyun begins to incorporate barbed wire and other industrial materials into his work.

1974 The first Seoul Biennale, organized by AG, opens at the National Museum of Modern and Contemporary Art, Korea.

Ha Chong-Hyun begins his *Conjunction* series, presenting *Work 74-A* at Myung-Dong Gallery, Seoul, Korea.

1974–1977
Ha Chong-Hyun begins to use the color white exclusively in his *Conjunction* series.

1975 Kwon Young-Woo, Park Seo-Bo, Suh Seung-Won, Lee Dong-Youb, and Hur Hwang participate in *Five Korean Artists, Five Kinds of White* held at Tokyo Gallery, Japan. The group exhibition is regarded as the beginning of the Dansaekhwa movement.

The École de Seoul and Seoul Contemporary Arts Festival are established to present major Dansaekhwa paintings.

1977 Ha Chong-Hyun participates in the 14th São Paulo Bienal.

Ha Chong-Hyun begins to introduce shades of khaki and golden brown.

1980 The May 18 Gwangju Uprising challenges General Chun Doo Hwan's military dictatorship. Chun brutally suppresses the movement and becomes president of South Korea.

1980s The Minjung art (people's art) movement begins; it will peak during the 1980s.

Early 1980s
Ha Chong-Hyun begins using what he describes as "a dark blue, bordering on black" tone in his paintings.

1987 The June Democratic Uprising leads to the establishment of direct presidential elections in South Korea.

1988 Seoul hosts the twenty-fourth Summer Olympic Games.

1993 **Ha Chong-Hyun represents Korea at the 45th Venice Biennale in Venice, Italy.**

1990–1994
Ha Chong-Hyun serves as dean of the College of Fine Arts at Hongik University.

1995 The Korean Pavilion is established at the 46th Venice Biennale. The 1st Gwangju Biennale is held.

2000 Ha Chong-Hyun's work is included in *The Facets of Korean and Japanese Contemporary Art* in the 3rd Gwangju Biennale.

2001 *Ha Chong-Hyun: 1986–2001* opens at Kamakura Gallery, Tokyo, Japan.

2001–2006
Ha Chong-Hyun serves as director of the Seoul Museum of Art.

2003 Ha Chong-Hyun has a solo exhibition at the Mudima Foundation for Contemporary Art, Milan, Italy.

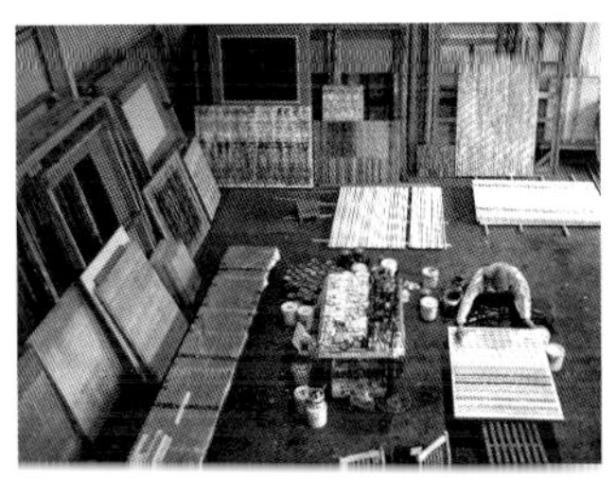

Ha Chong-Hyun in his studio.

2004 Ha Chong-Hyun has a solo exhibition at Gyeongnam Art Museum, Changwon, Korea.

2010 Ha Chong-Hyun begins his *Post Conjunction* series.

2012 Ha Chong-Hyun retrospective takes place at the National Museum of Modern and Contemporary Art, Gwacheon.

2015 Ha Chong-Hyun's work is included in *Dansaekhwa*, a collateral exhibition at the Palazzo Contarini Polignac as part of the 56th Venice Biennale.

2018 Ha Chong-Hyun's work is included in *Korean Abstract Art: Kim Whanki and Dansaekhwa*, Powerlong Museum, Shanghai, China.

2019 Ha Chong-Hyun's work is exhibited in *War Within, War Without, Collection 1940s–1970s*, Museum of Modern Art, New York, United States.

2020 Ha Chong-Hyun has a solo exhibition at the Daejeon Museum of Art, Korea.

2022 Ha Chong-Hyun's solo collateral exhibition opens at Palazzetto Tito, in partnership with Fondazione Bevilacqua La Masa, as part of the 59th Venice Biennale.

SELECTED WORKS

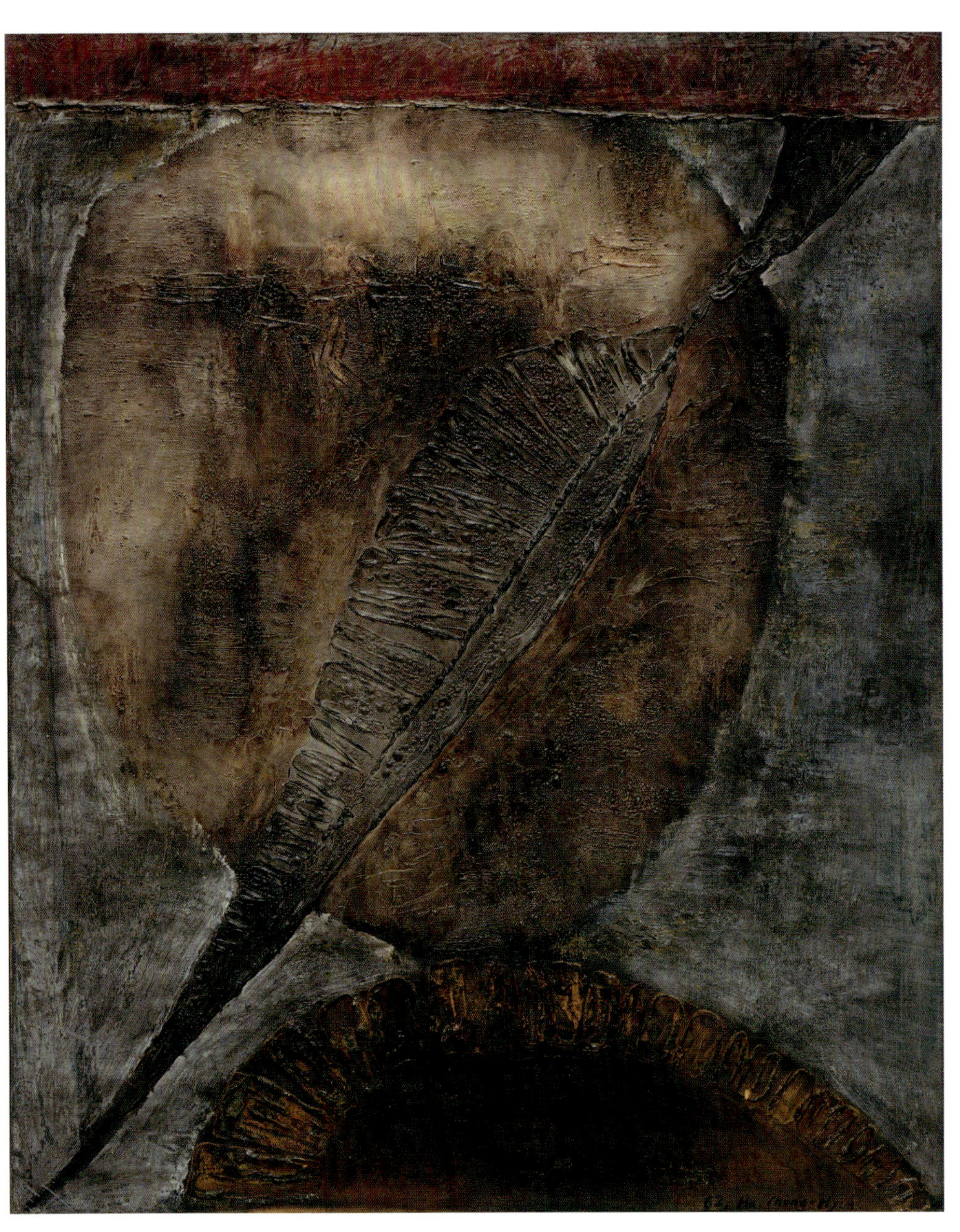

 Work C, 1962. Oil and collage on canvas, 63 3/4 x 51 1/2 inches (162 x 130 cm)

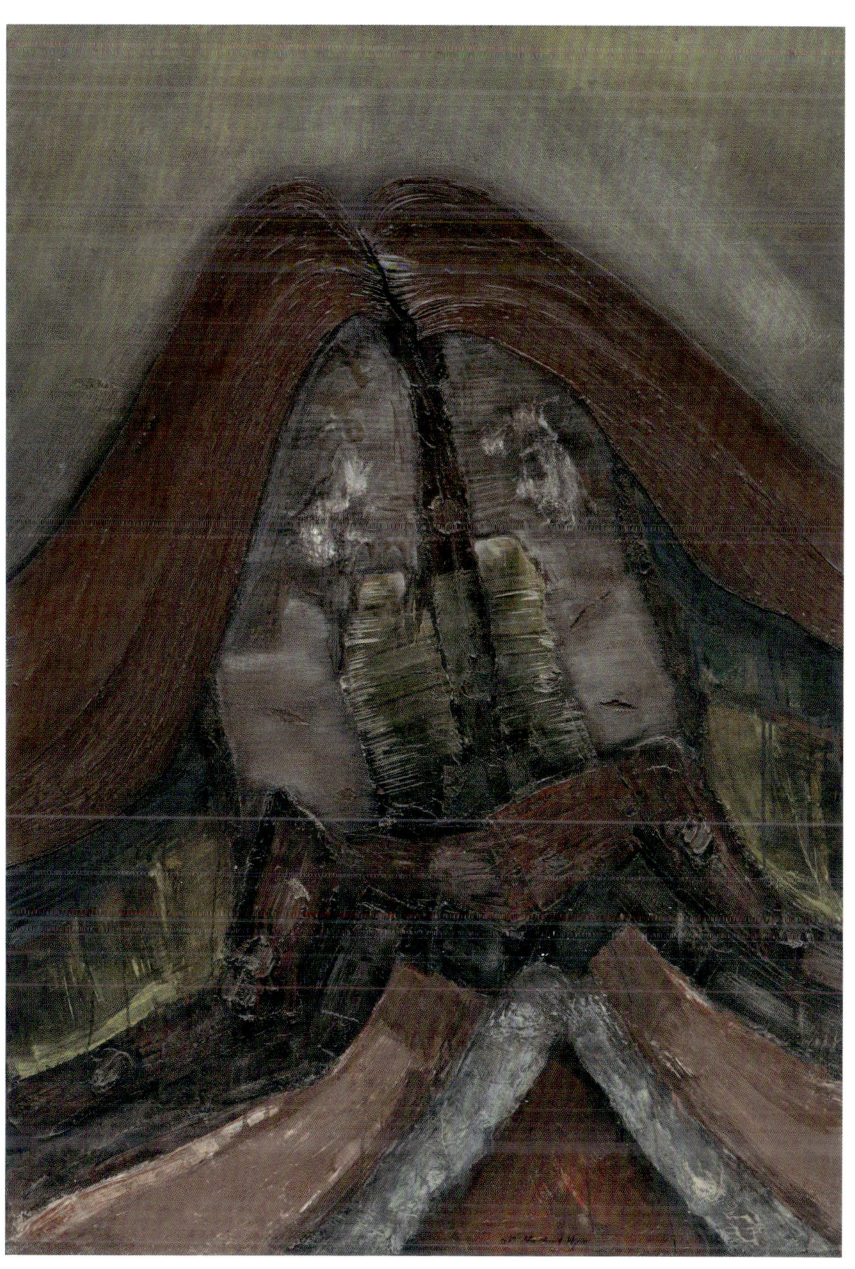

 Amulette-A, 1965. Oil and collage on canvas, 64 1/5 x 44 1/2 inches (163 x 113 cm)

Naissance 67, 1967. Oil and collage on canvas, 37 x 37 inches (94 x 94 cm)

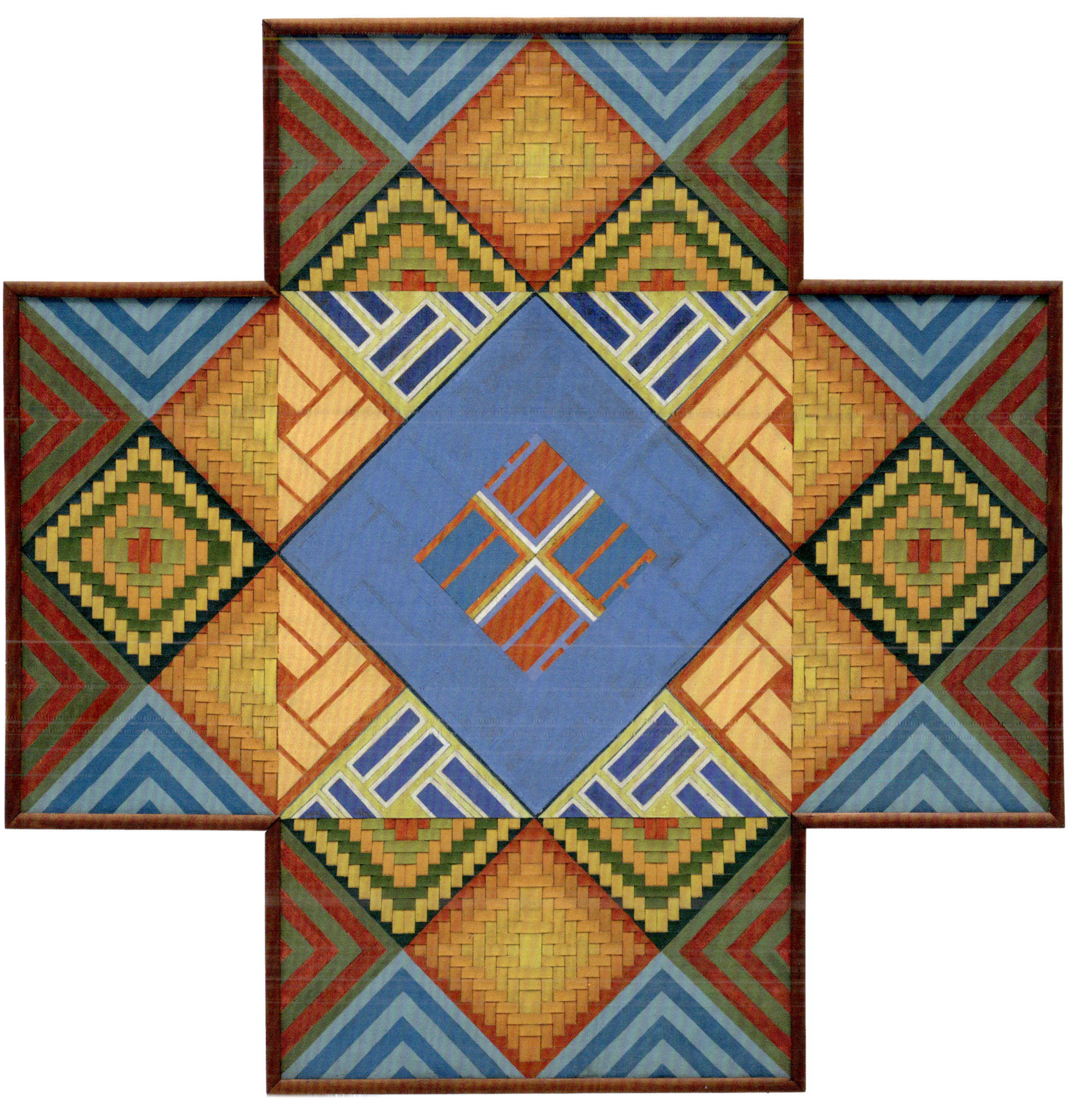

Naissance-B, 1967. Oil and collage on canvas, 57 1/3 x 76 1/3 inches (145.5 x 193.9 cm)

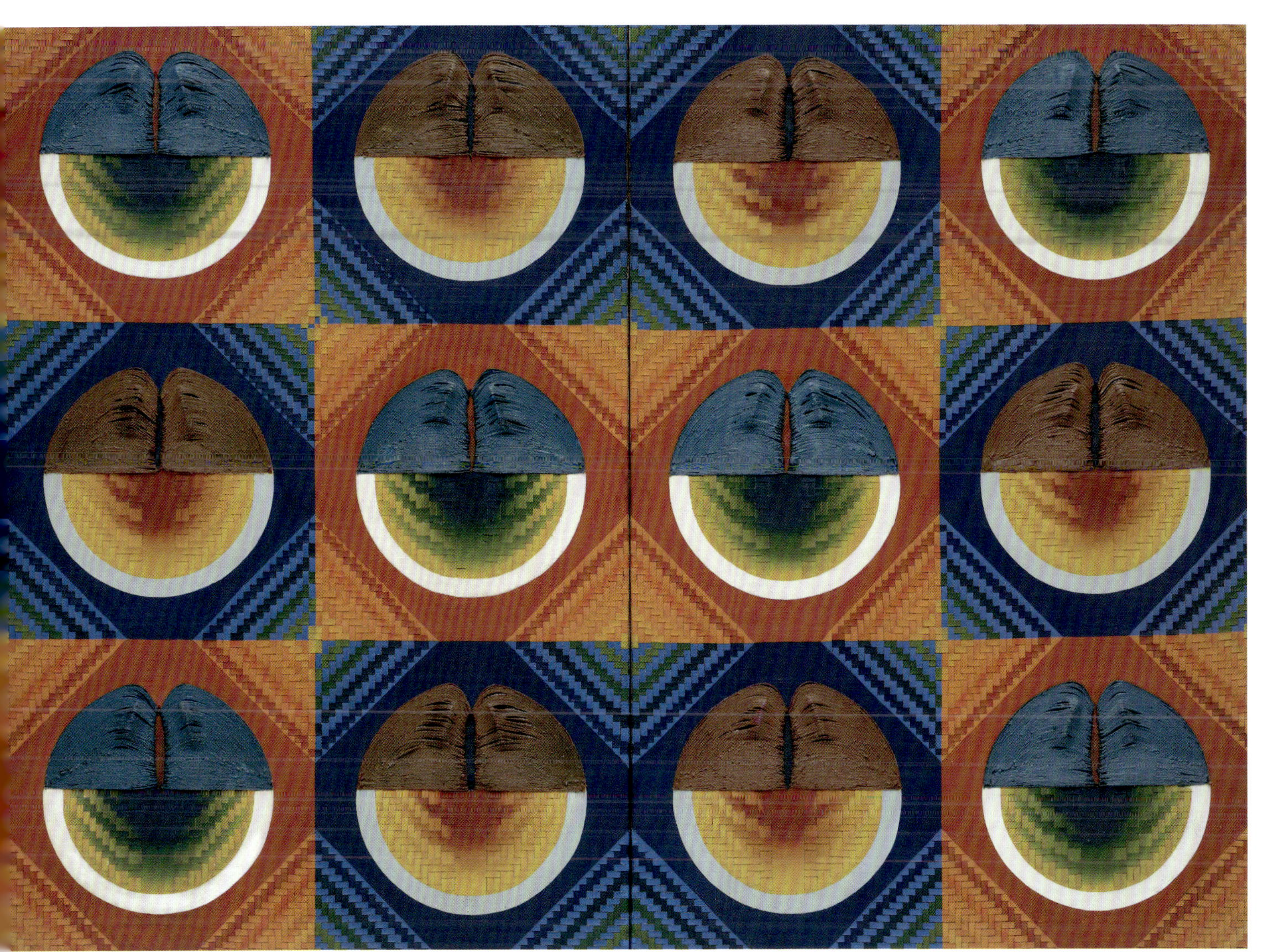

White Paper on Urban Planning, 1967. Oil on canvas, 44 1/8 x 44 1/8 inches (112 x 112 cm)

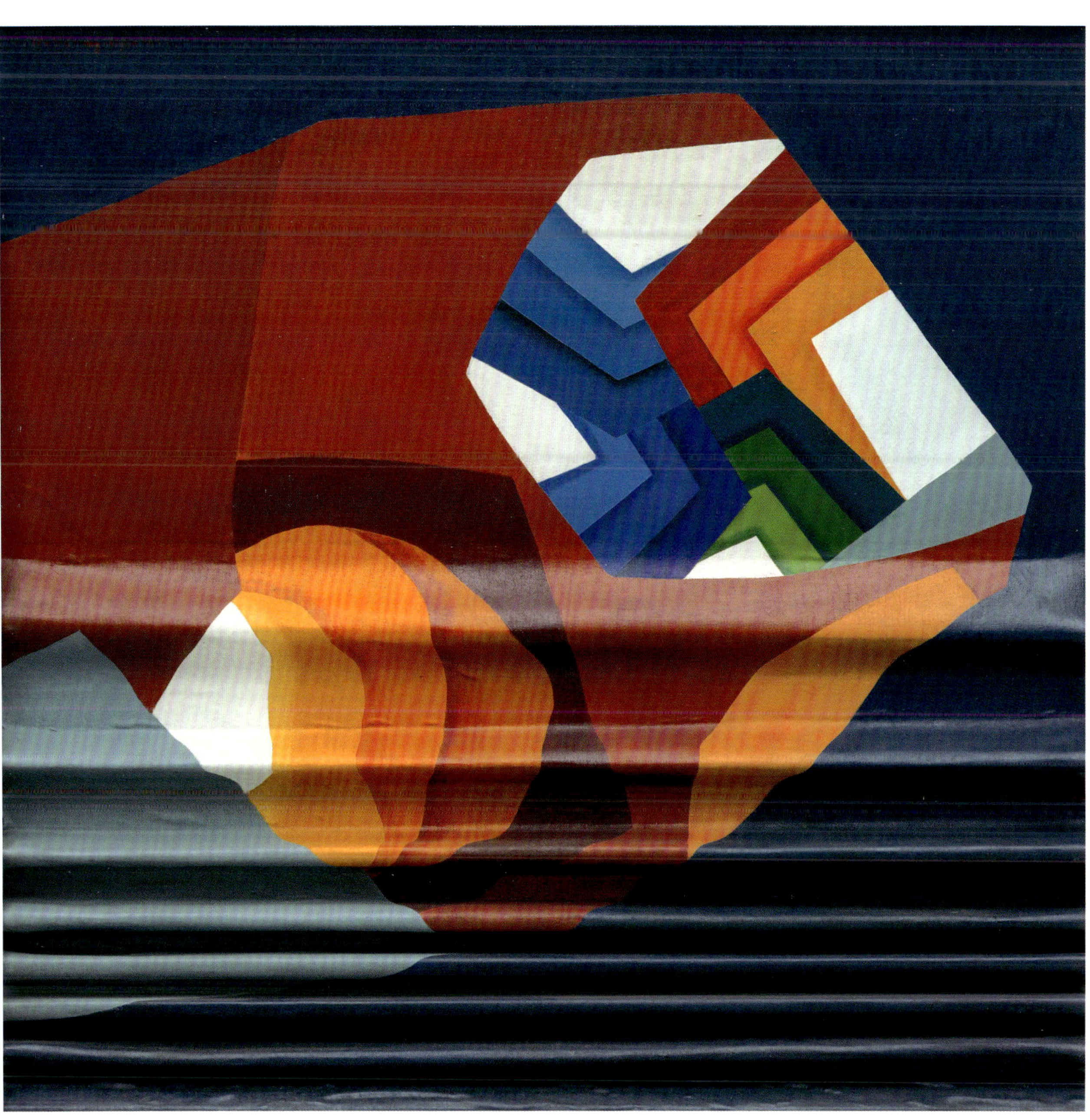

White Paper on Urban Planning 68, 1968. Oil on canvas, 47 1/4 x 47 1/4 inches (120 x 120 cm)

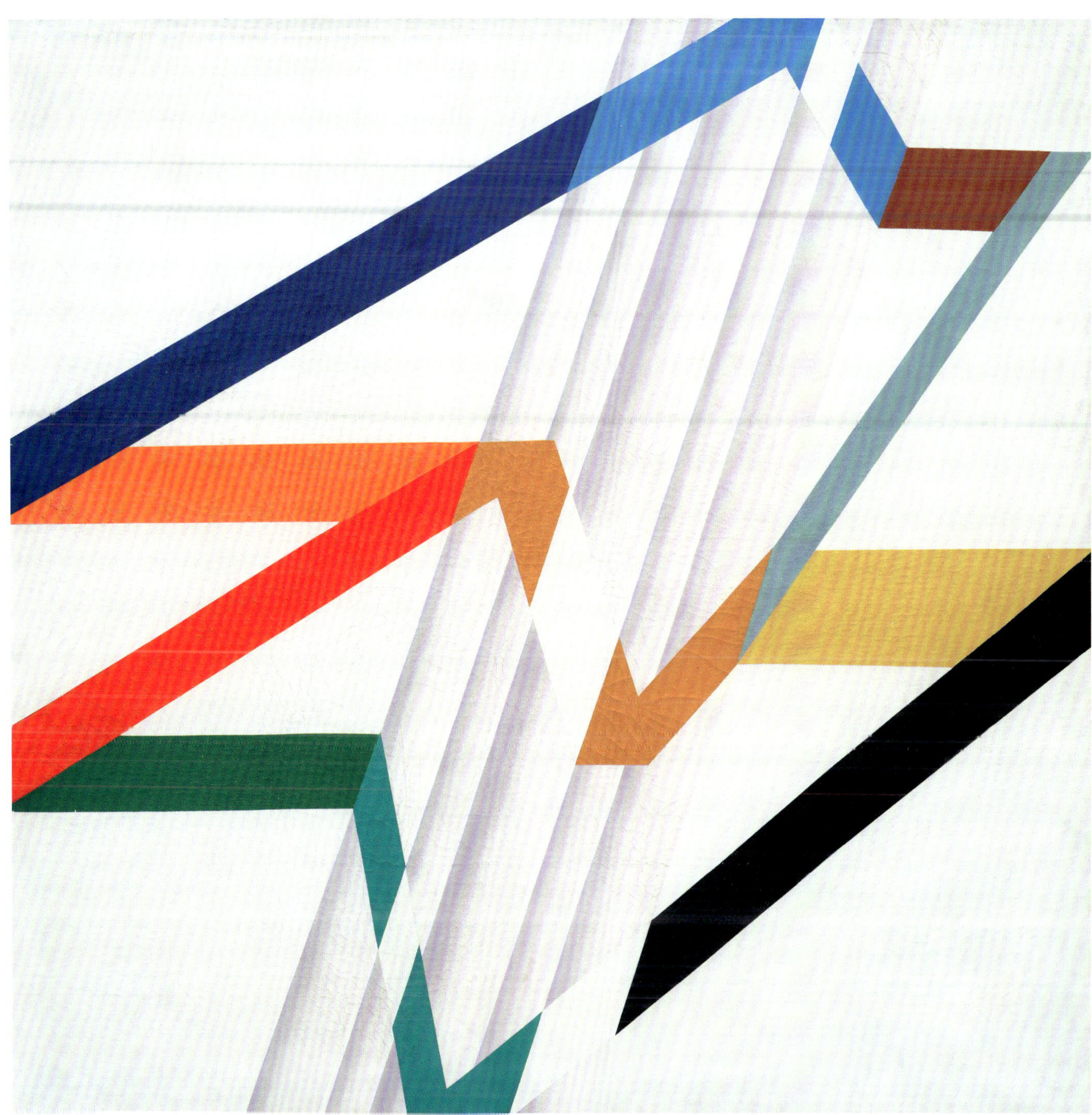

White Paper on Urban Planning No.1, 1968. Oil on canvas, 41 1/3 x 41 1/3 inches (105 x 105cm)

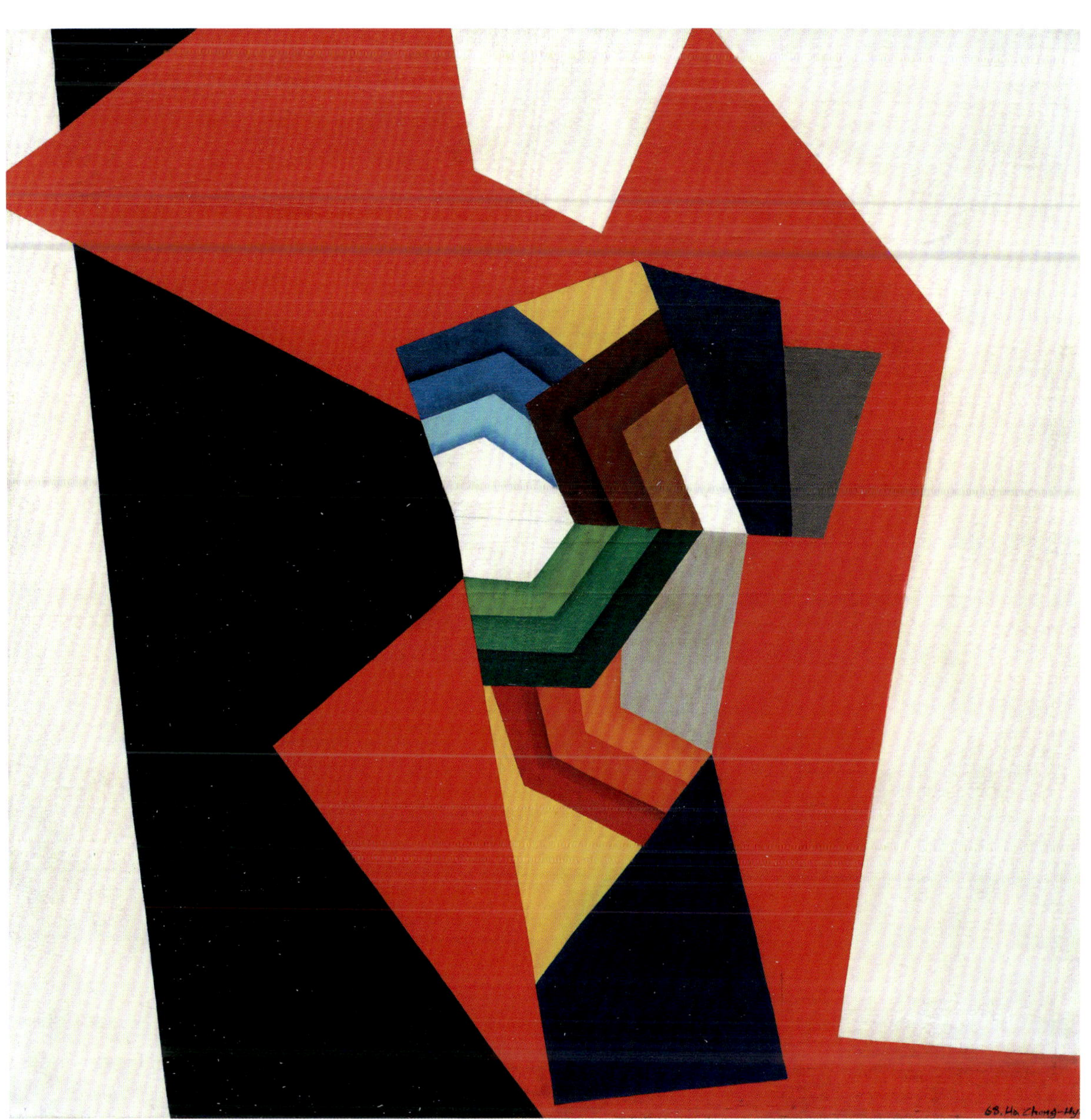
68. Ha Zhong-Hy

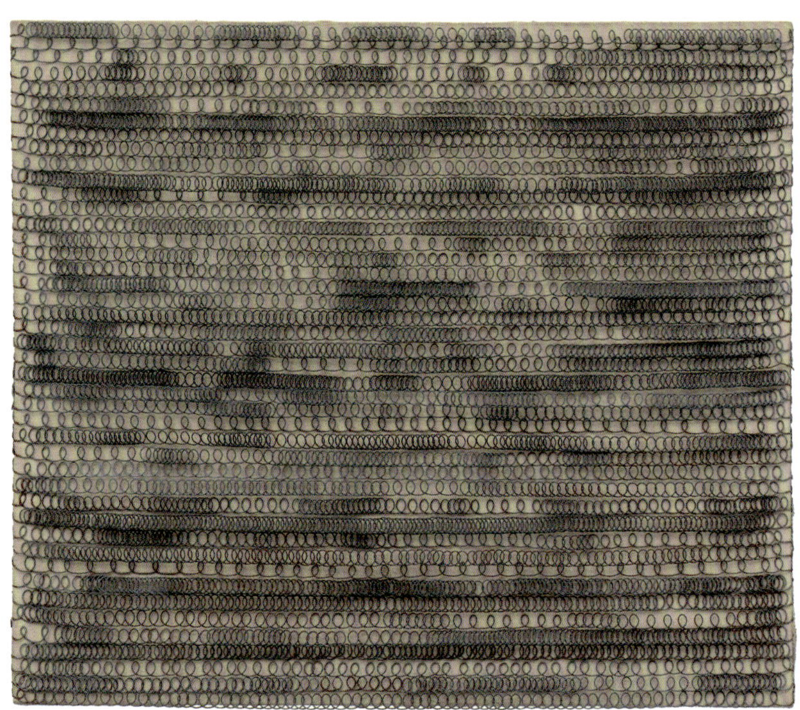

Work 73, 1973. Metal springs on canvas, 18 x 20 7/8 inches (45.5 x 53 cm)

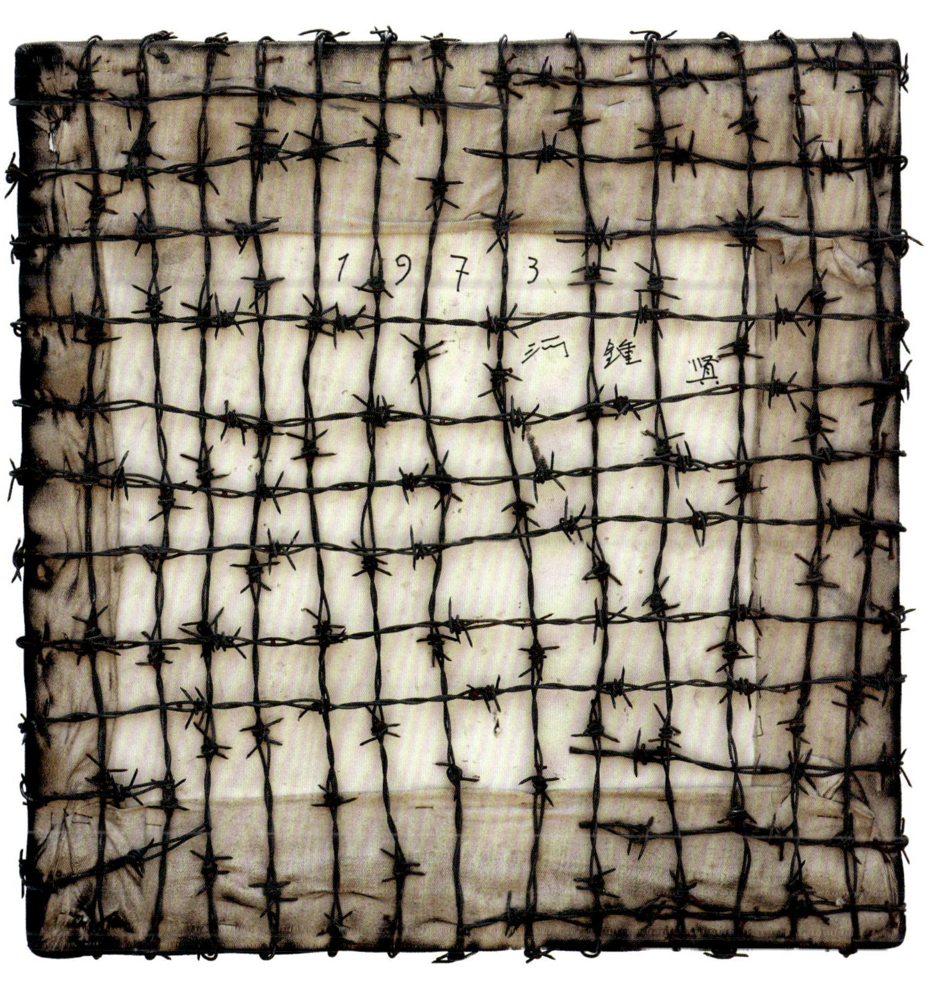

 Work 73, 1973. Barbed wire on panel, 23 5/8 x 23 5/8 inches (60 x 60 cm)

Untitled 72-3(B), 1972. Metal springs on panel, 29 1/8 x 59 1/8 inches (74 x 150 cm)

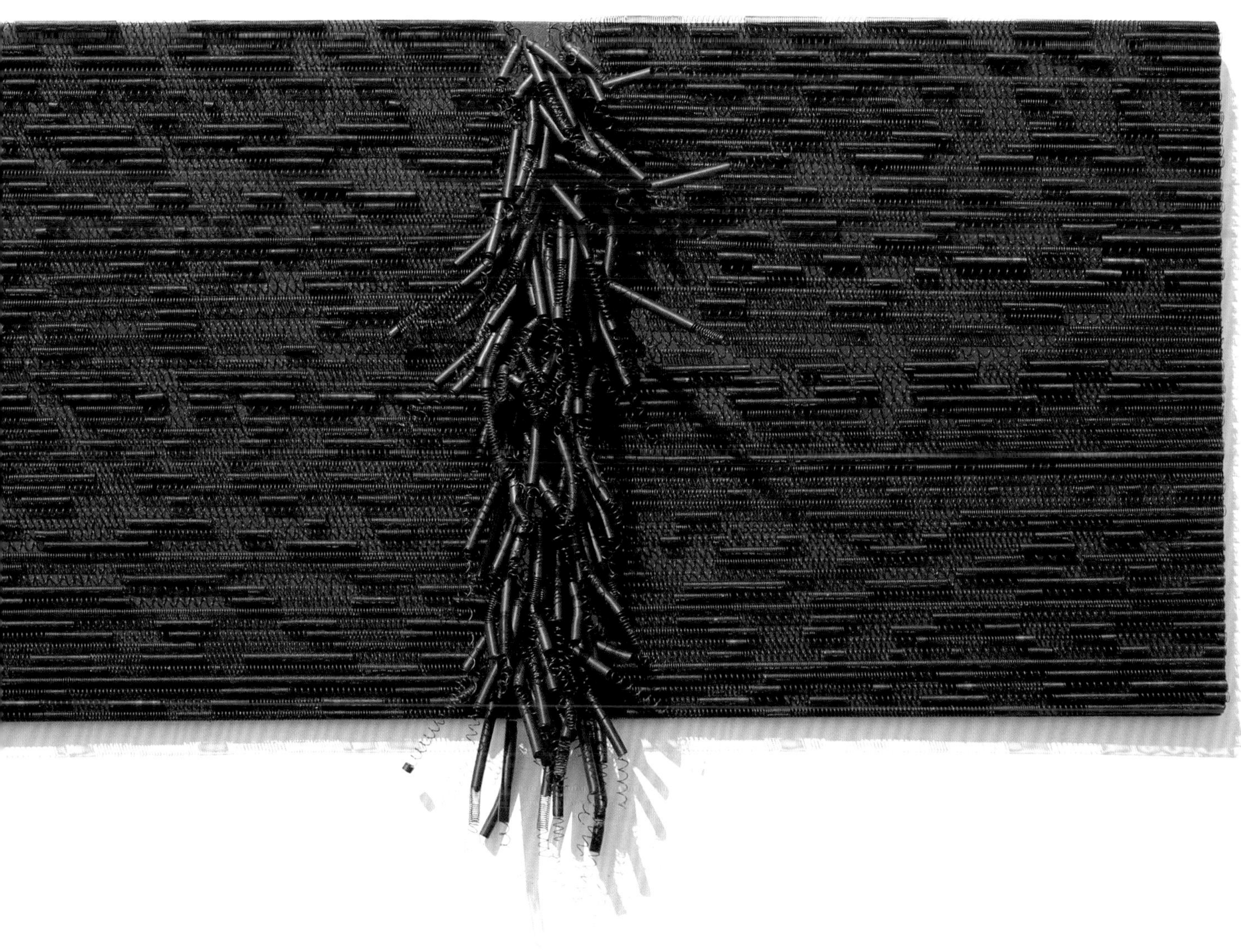

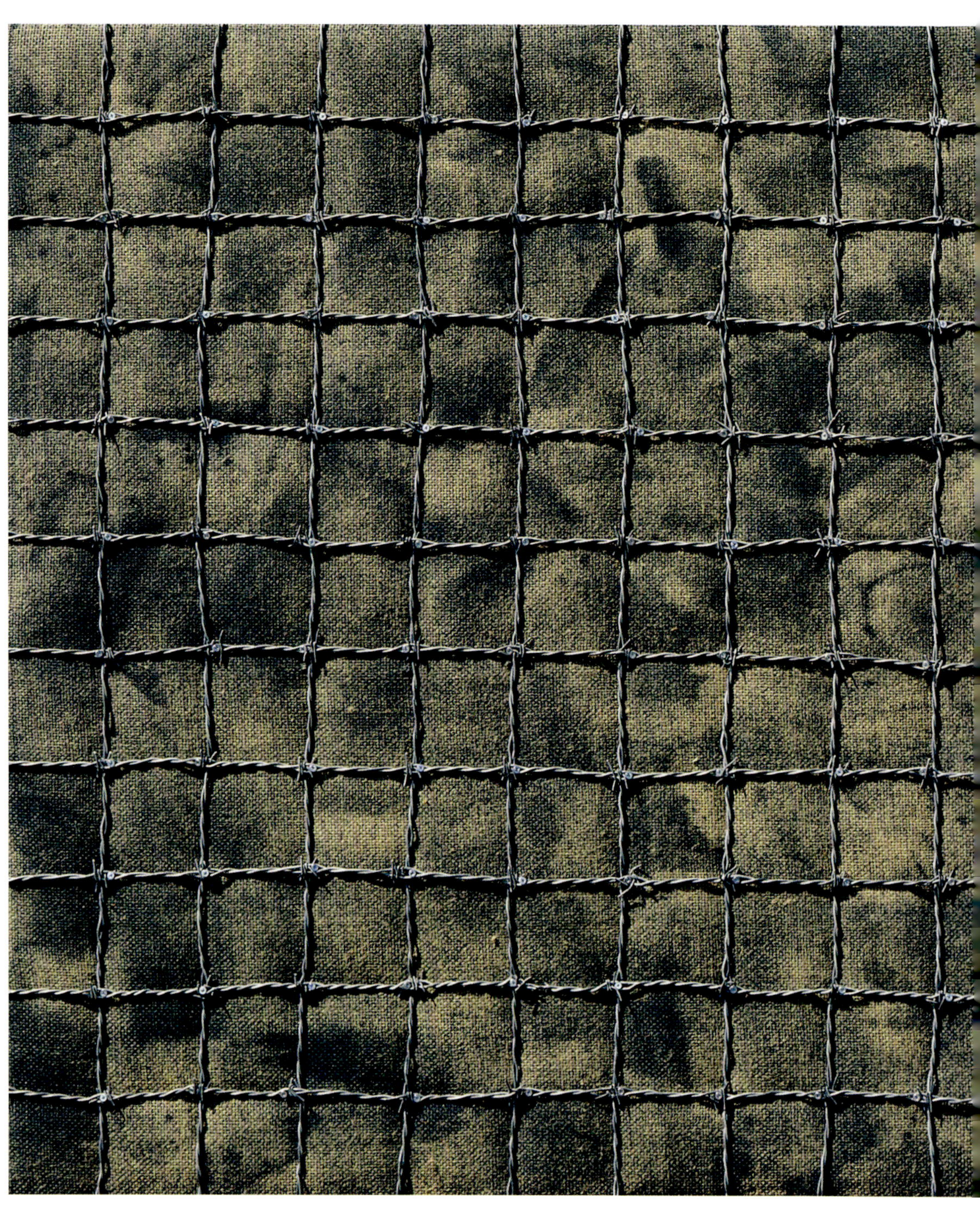

 Work 73-13, 1973. Barbed wire on hemp, 47 1/4 x 94 1/2 inches (120 x 240 cm)

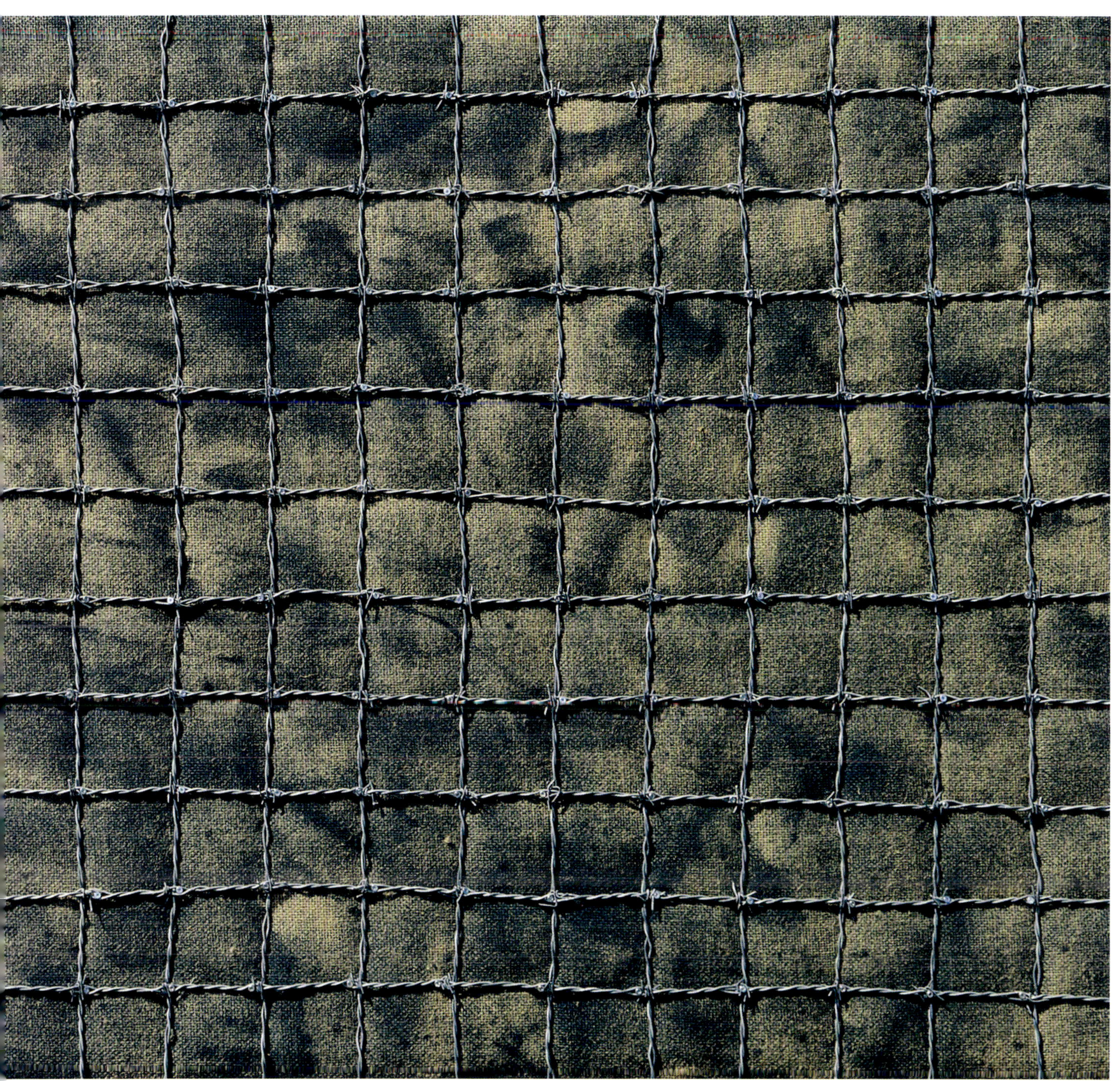

 Untitled 73-2(A), 1973. Spring on panel, 48 1/8 x 96 1/8 inches (122 x 244 cm)

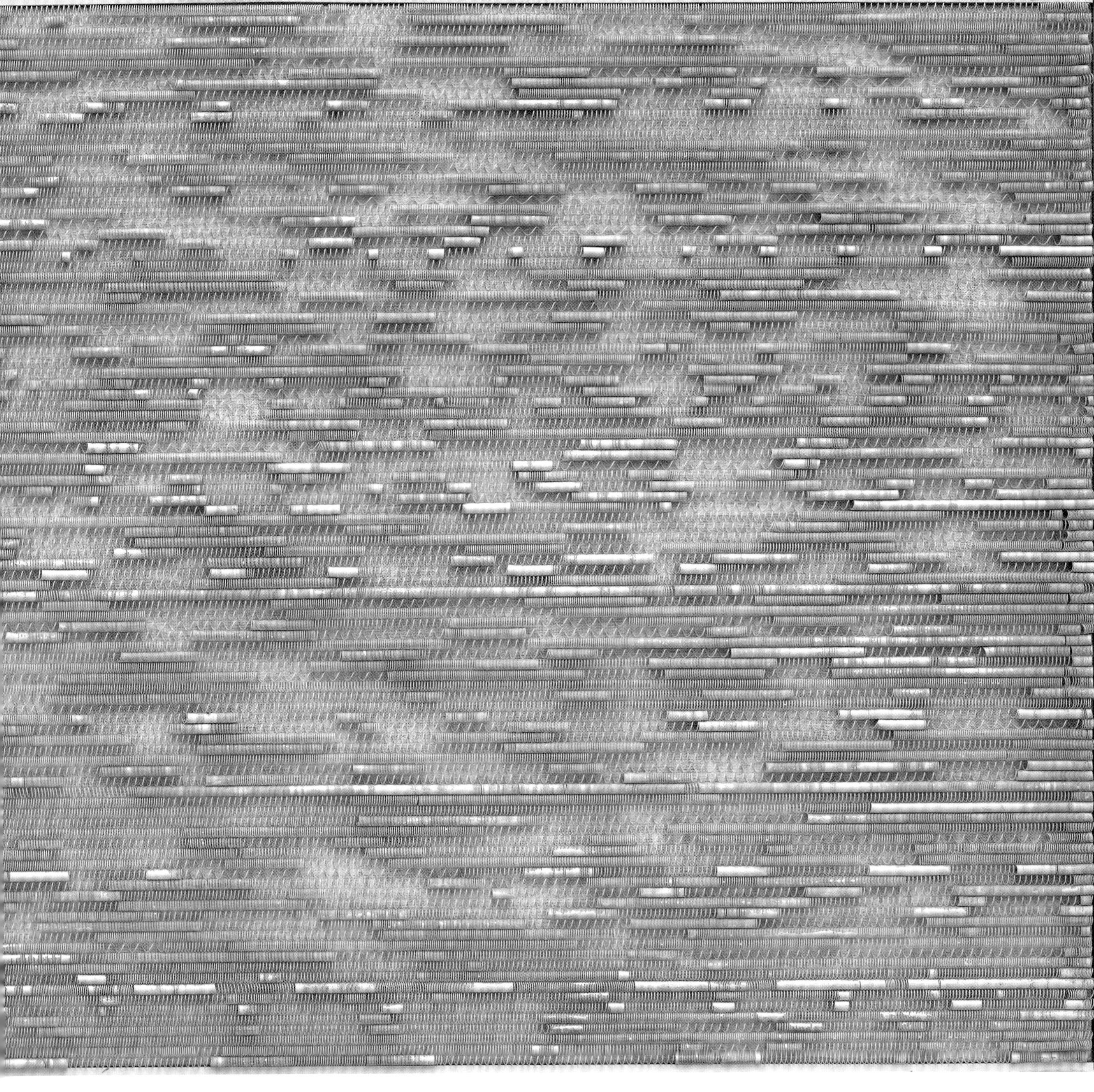

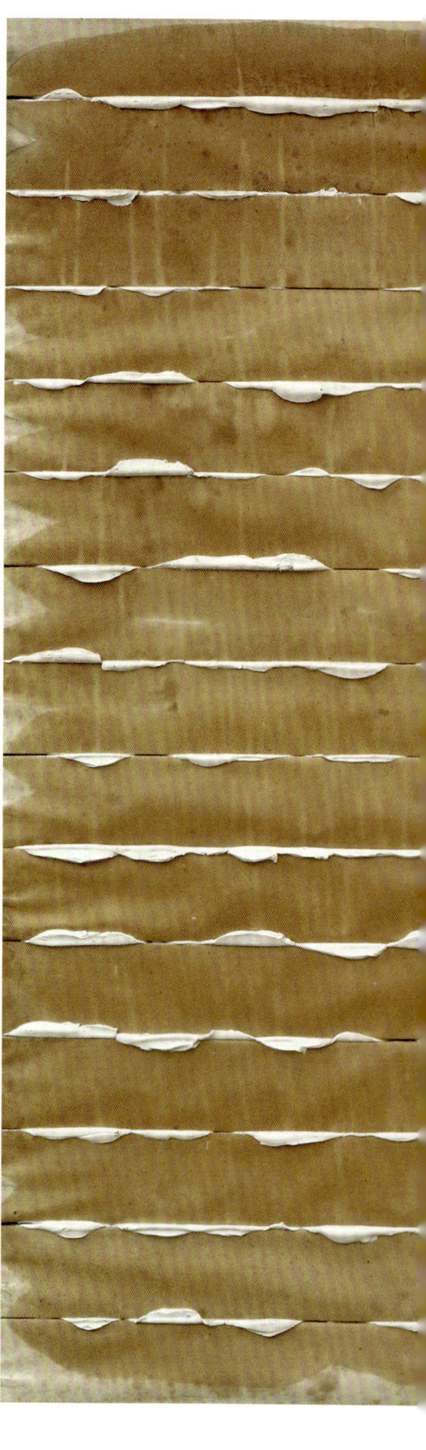

Conjunction, 1974. Oil on paper, 47 1/4 x 69 in (120 x 175 cm)

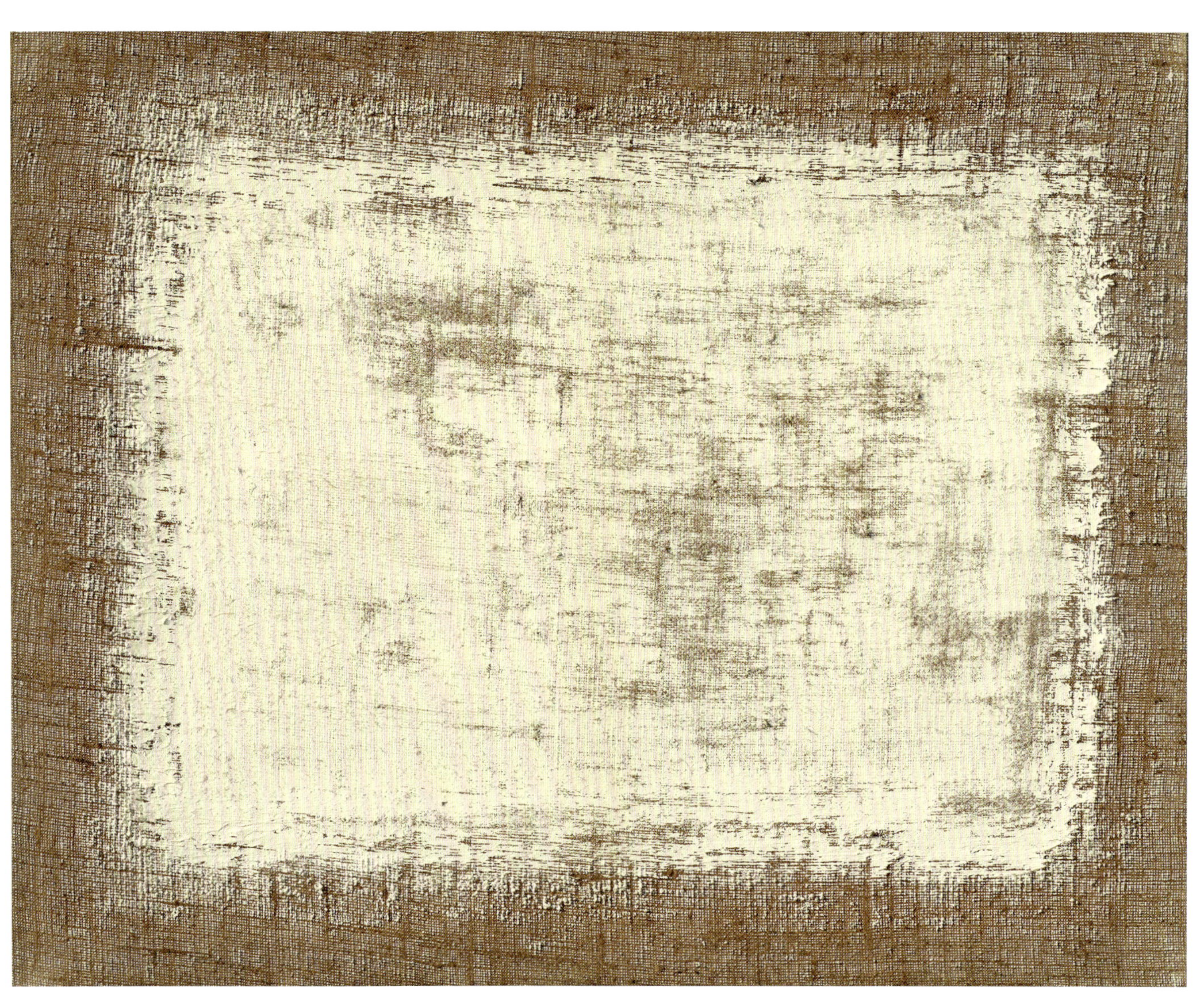

 Conjunction 74-17, 1974. Oil on hemp cloth, 31 1/2 x 39 2/5 inches (80 x 100 cm)

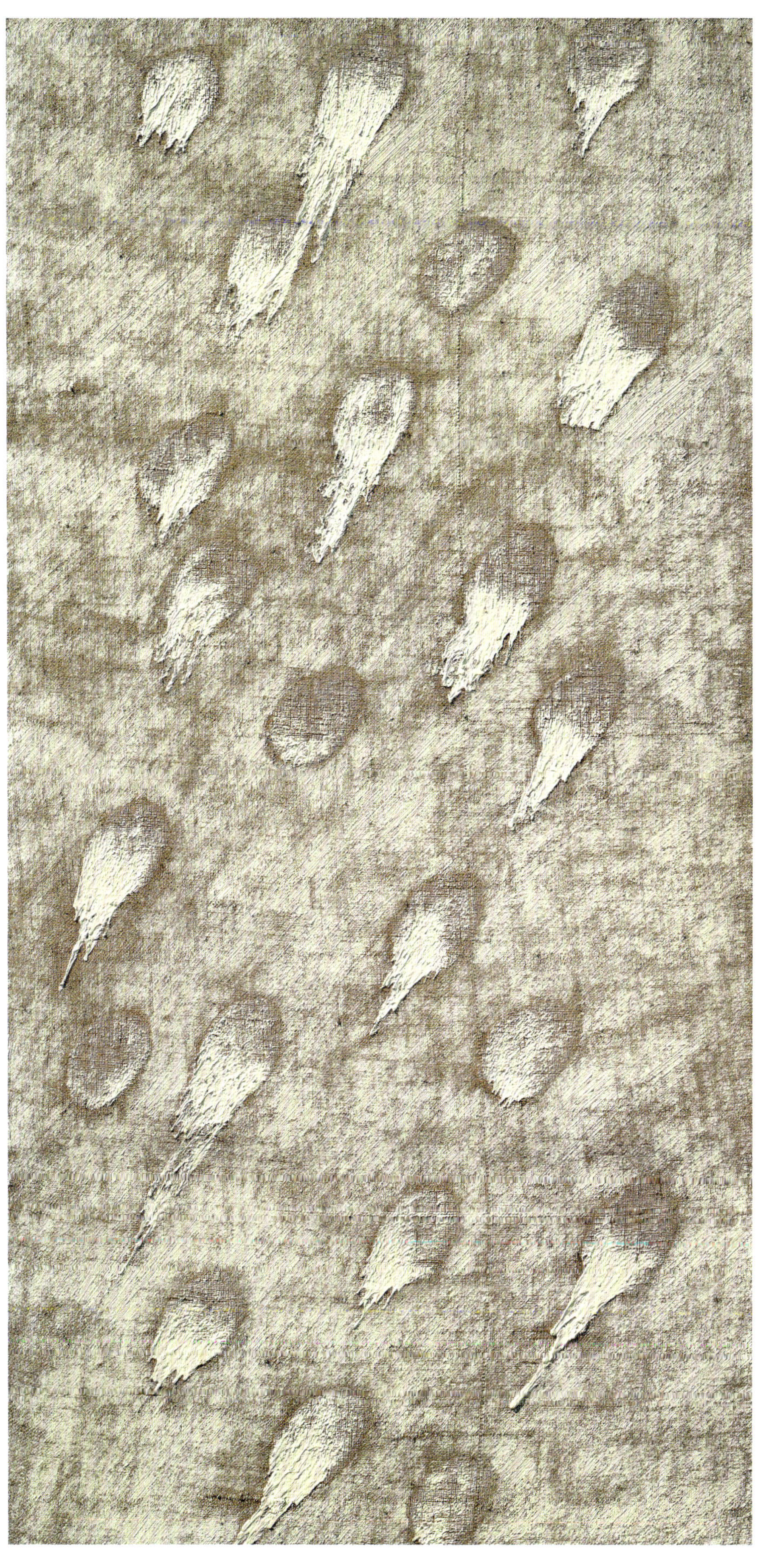

69 *Conjunction 74-24*, 1974. Oil on hemp cloth, 78 3/4 x 39 3/8 inches (200 x 100 cm)

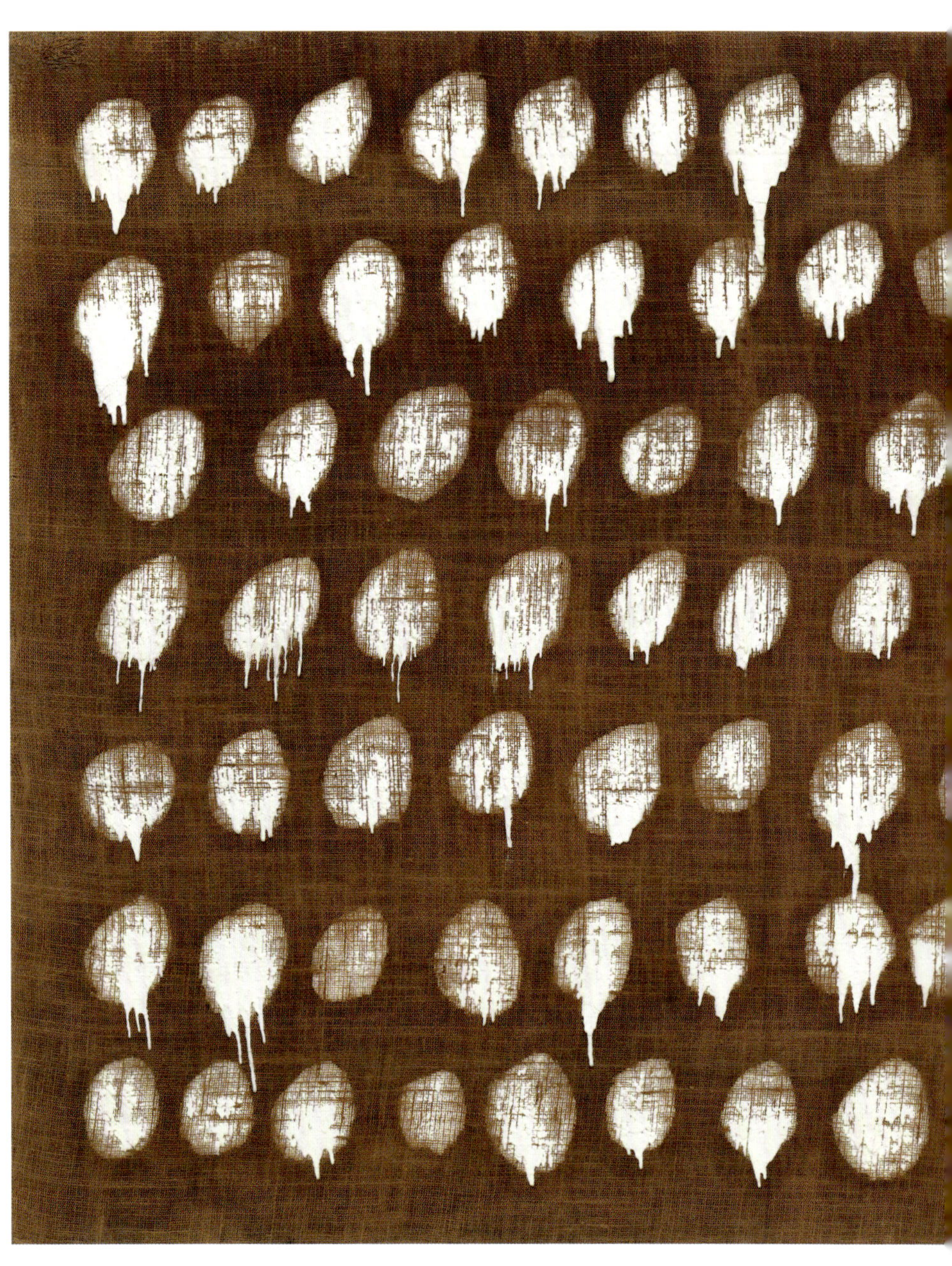

 Conjunction 74-26, 1974. Oil on burlap, 42 7/8 x 87 3/4 inches (108.9 x 222.9 cm)

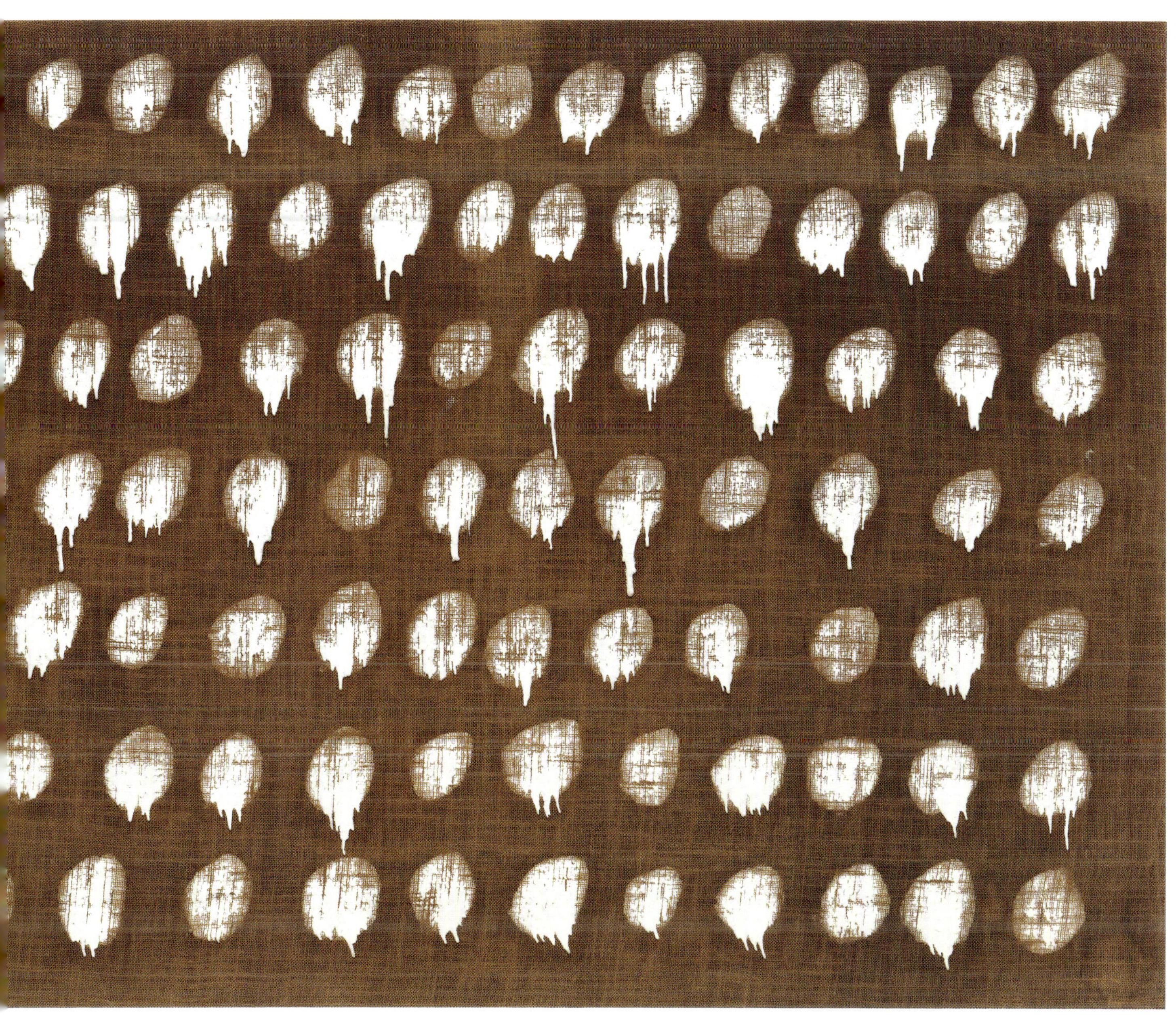

Conjunction 78-7, 1978. Oil on hemp cloth, 71 x 47 1/5 inches (179.8 × 120.5 cm)

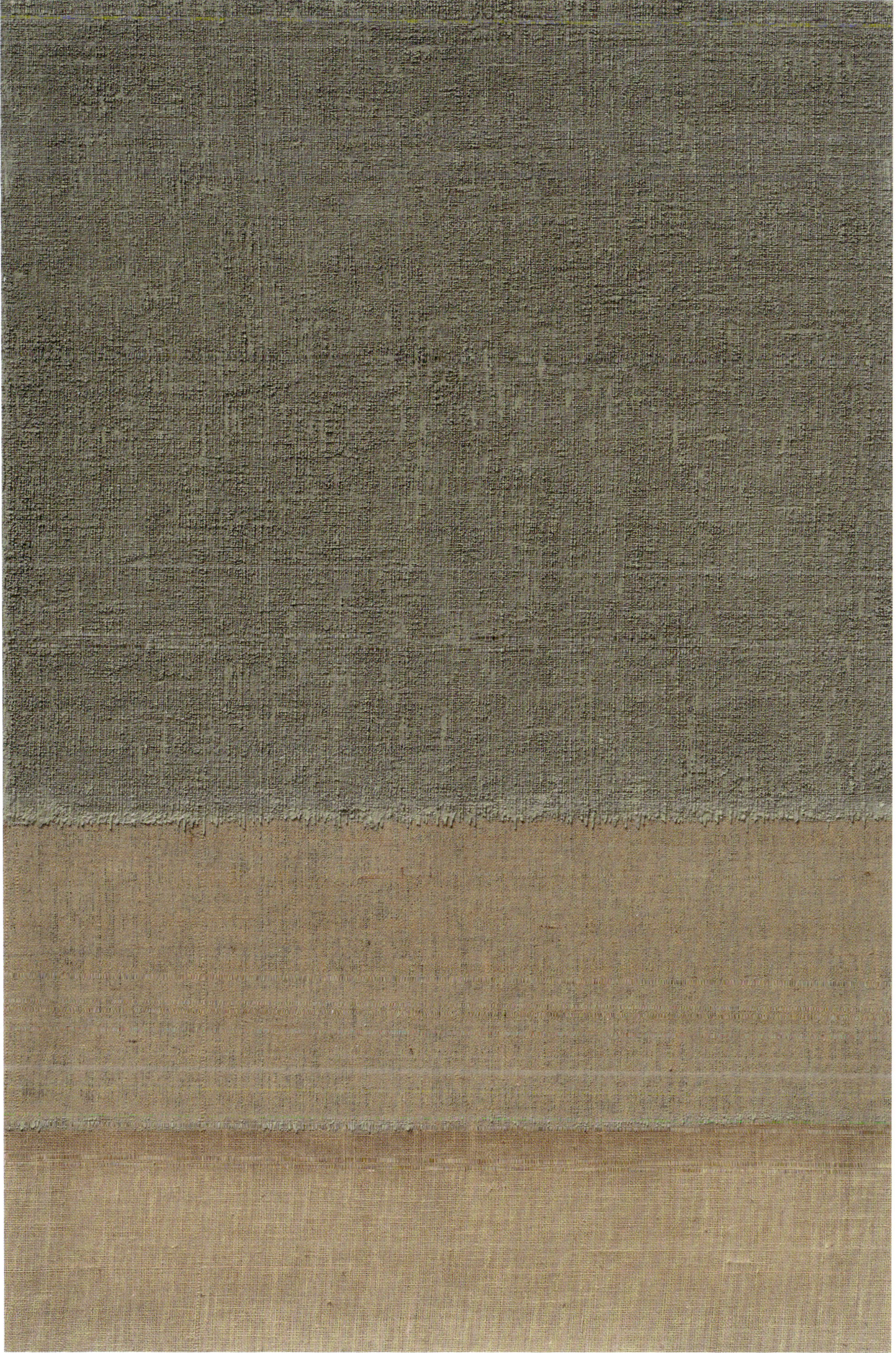

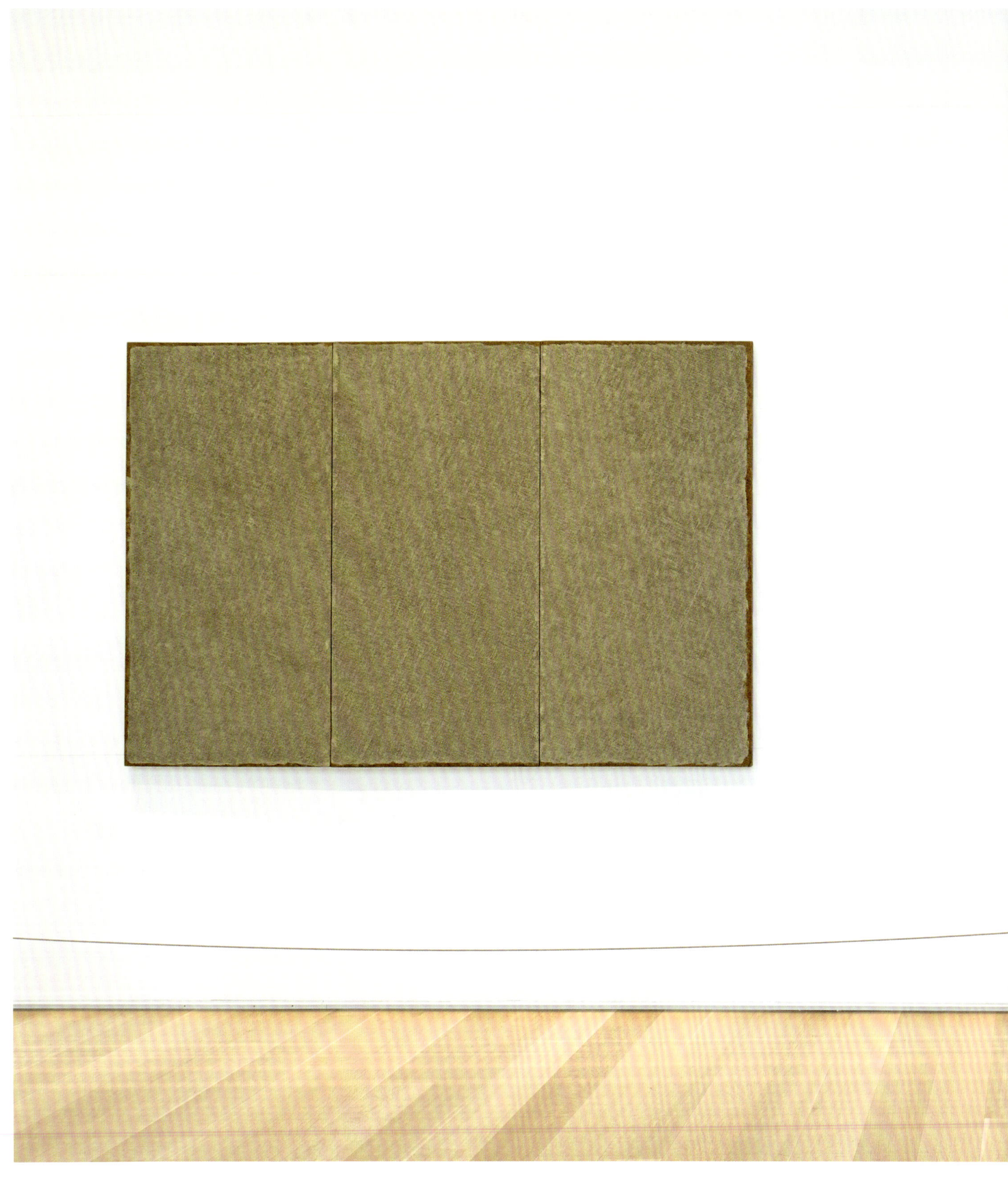

 Conjunction 79-31, 1979. Oil on hemp cloth, 59 1/8 x 89 inches (150 x 226 cm)

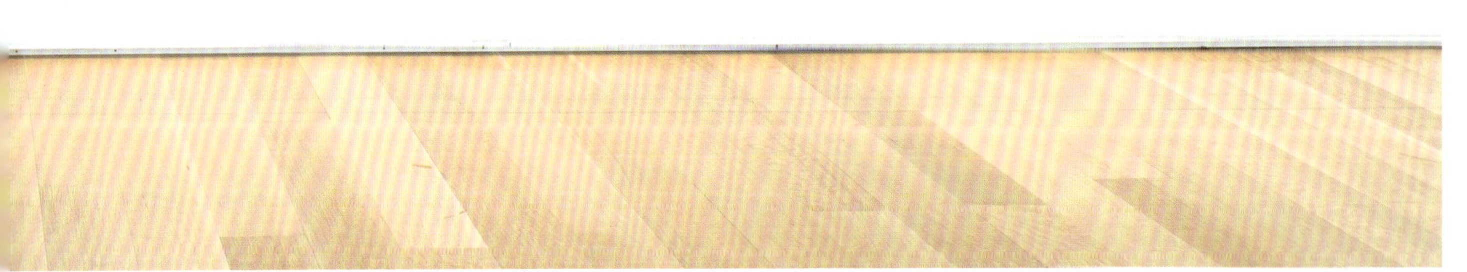

75 *Conjunction 81-79*, 1981. Oil on hemp cloth, 76 x 102 inches (194 x 260 cm)

Conjunction 83-08 (A+B), 1983. Oil on hemp cloth. Total: 86 5/8 x 86 5/8 inches (220 x 220 cm). Each panel: 86 5/8 x 43 5/16 inches (220 x 110 cm)

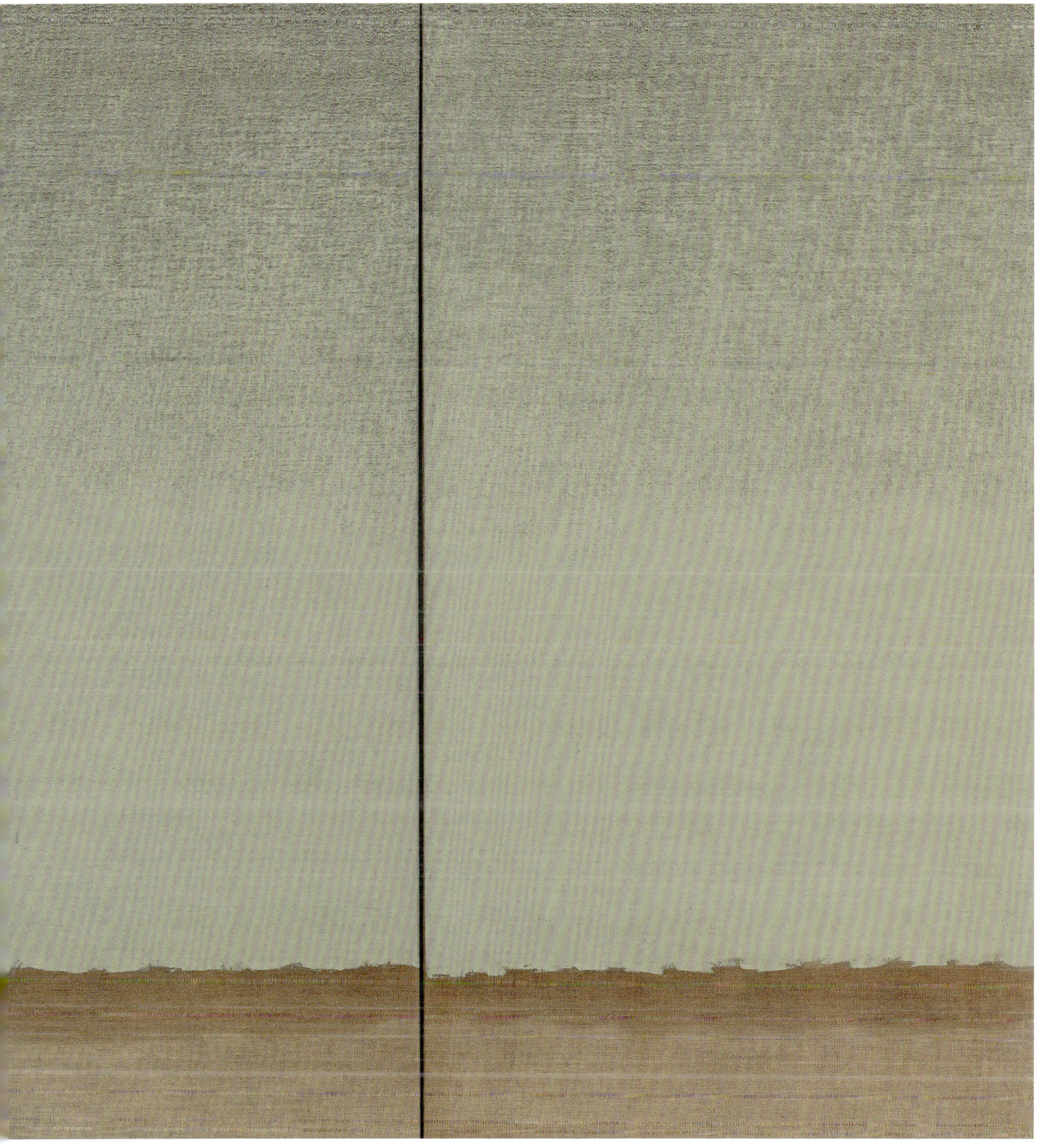

Conjunction 85-31, 1985. Oil on hemp cloth, 63 x 47 3/8 inches (160 x 120.3 cm)

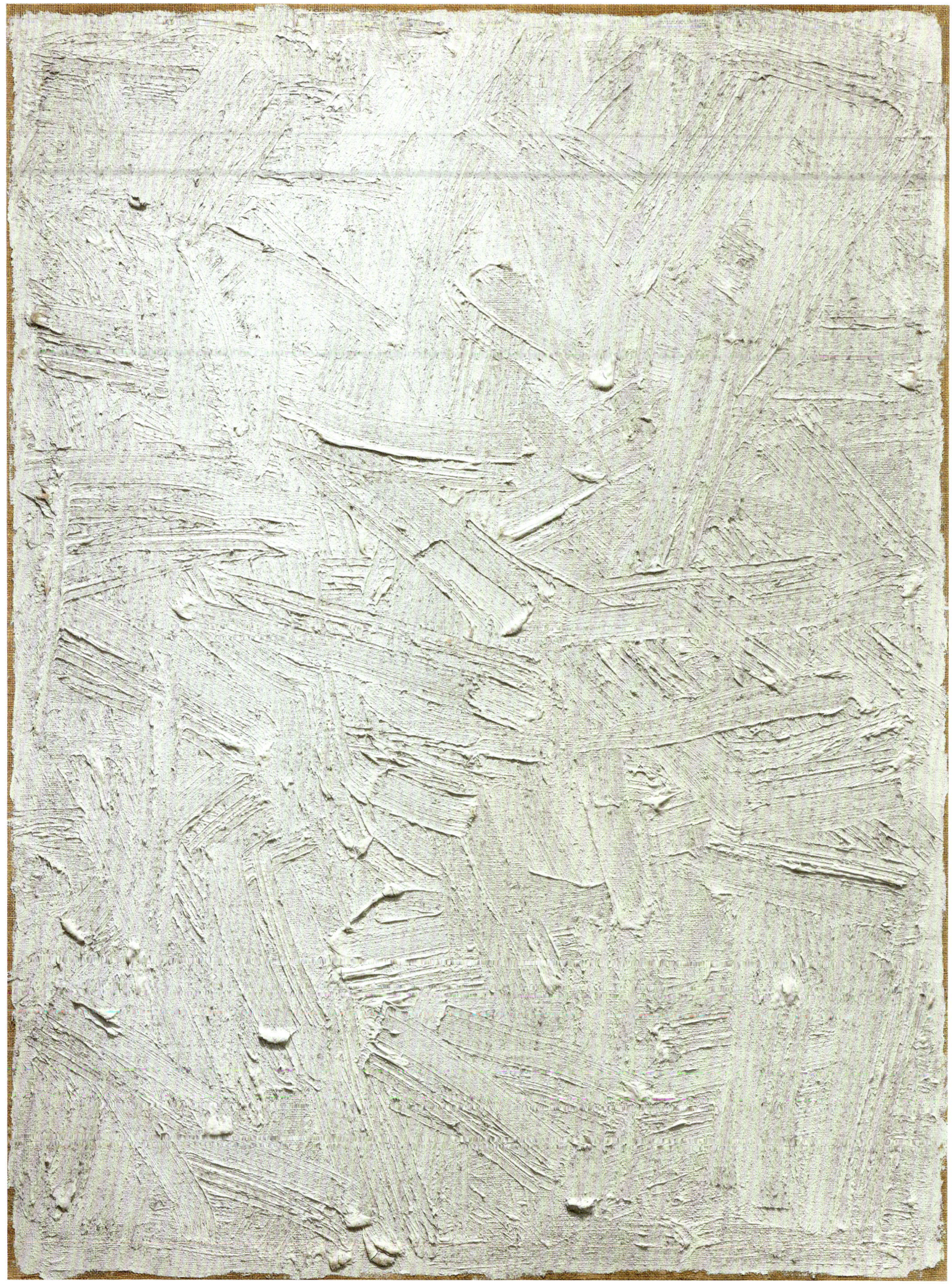

 Conjunction 92-24, 1992. Oil on hemp cloth, 47 1/4 x 47 1/4 inches (120 x 120 cm)

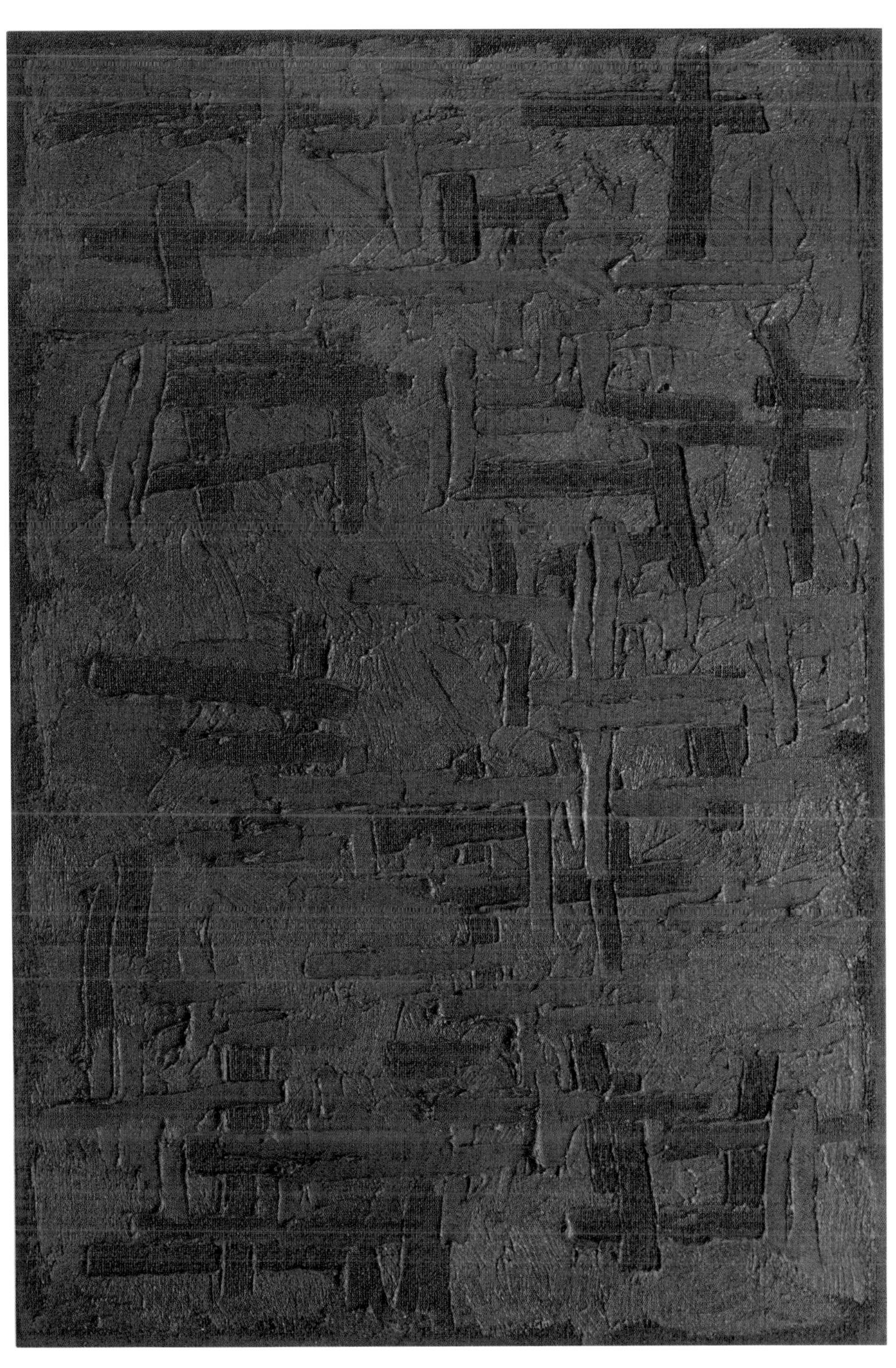

81 *Conjunction 97-002*, 1997. Oil on hemp cloth, 70 7/8 x 47 1/4 inches (180 x 120 cm)

Conjunction 95-021, 1995. Oil on hemp cloth, 72 7/8 x 72 7/8 inches (185 x 185 cm)

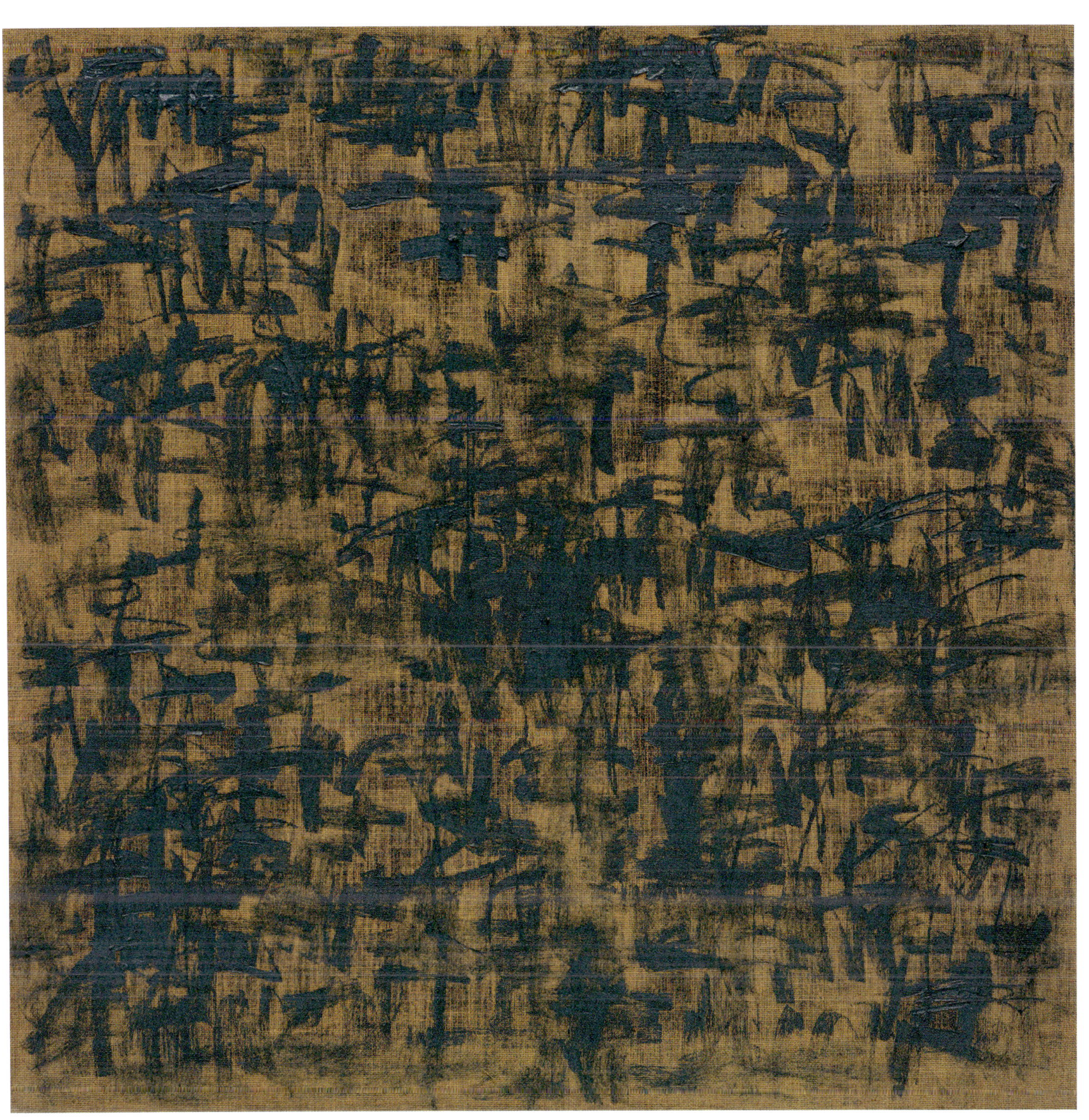

 Conjunction 98-203 (A) (B) (C), 1998. Oil on hemp cloth, 86 5/8 x 118 1/8 inches (220 x 300 cm)

 Conjunction 02-38 (B), 2004. Oil on hemp cloth, 102 3/8 x 76 3/8 inches (260 x 194 cm)

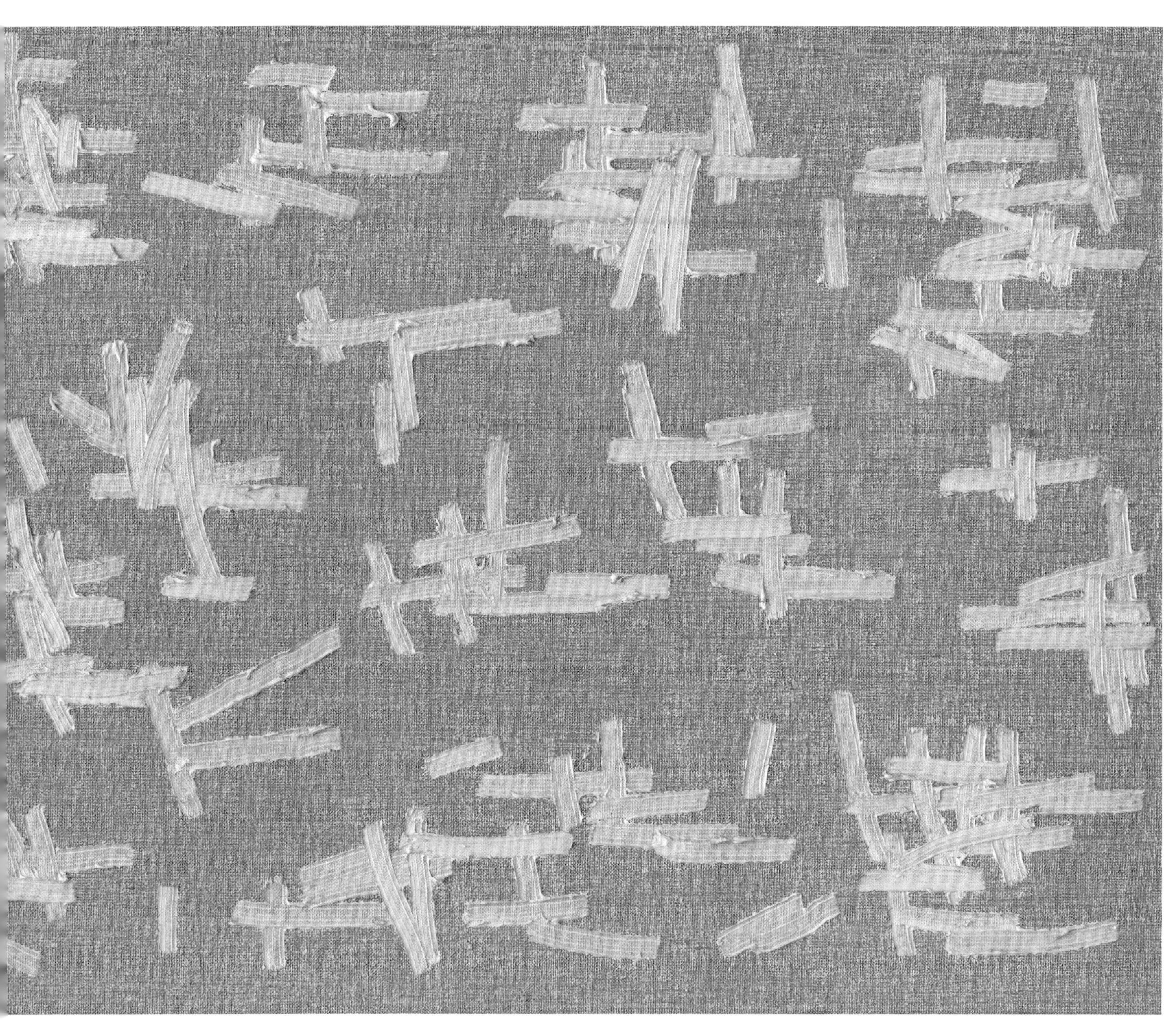

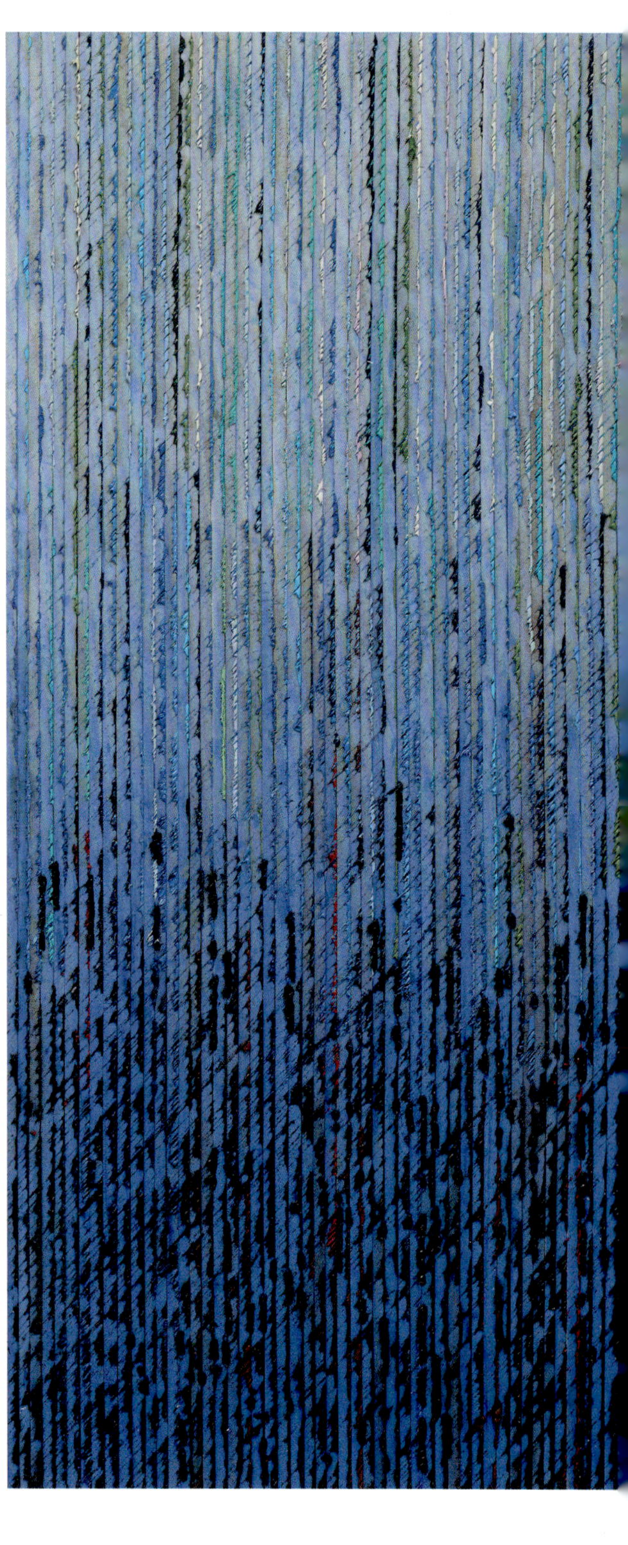

 Post Conjunction 10-2, 2010. Mixed media, 96 1/8 x 114 1/8 inches (244 x 366 cm)

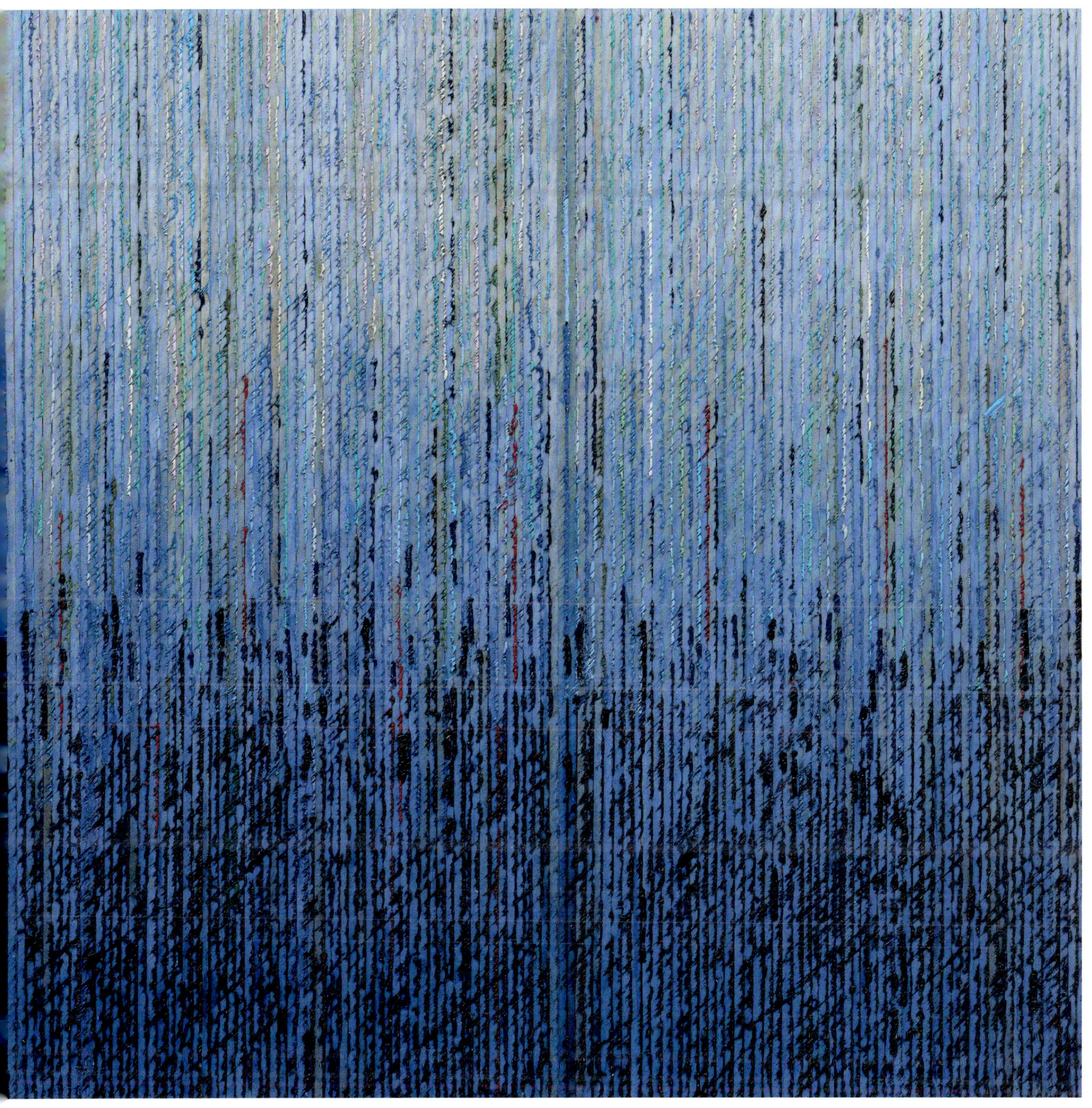

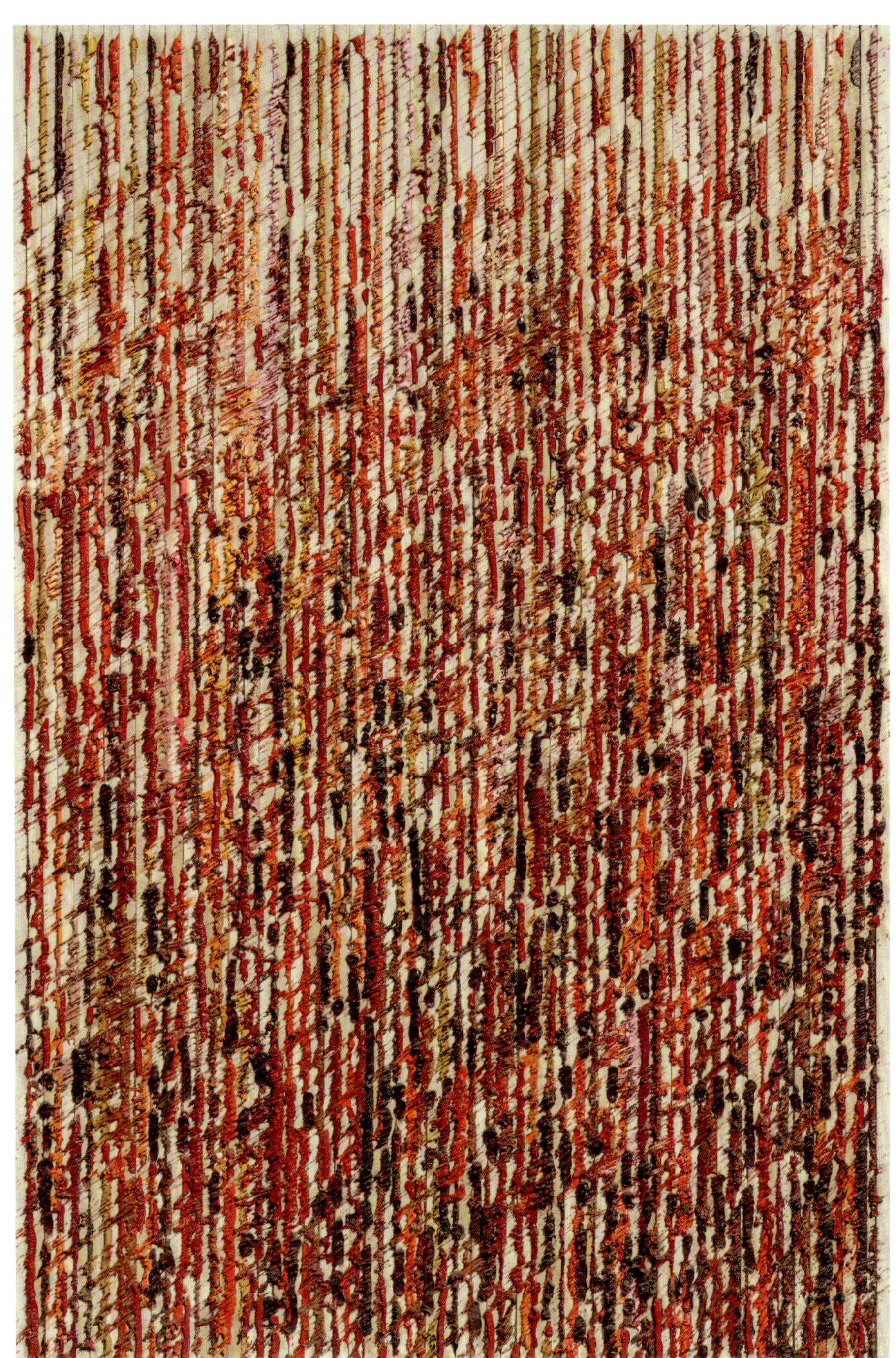

 Post Conjunction 10-(A), 2010. Mixed media, 70 7/8 x 47 1/4 inches (180 x 120 cm)

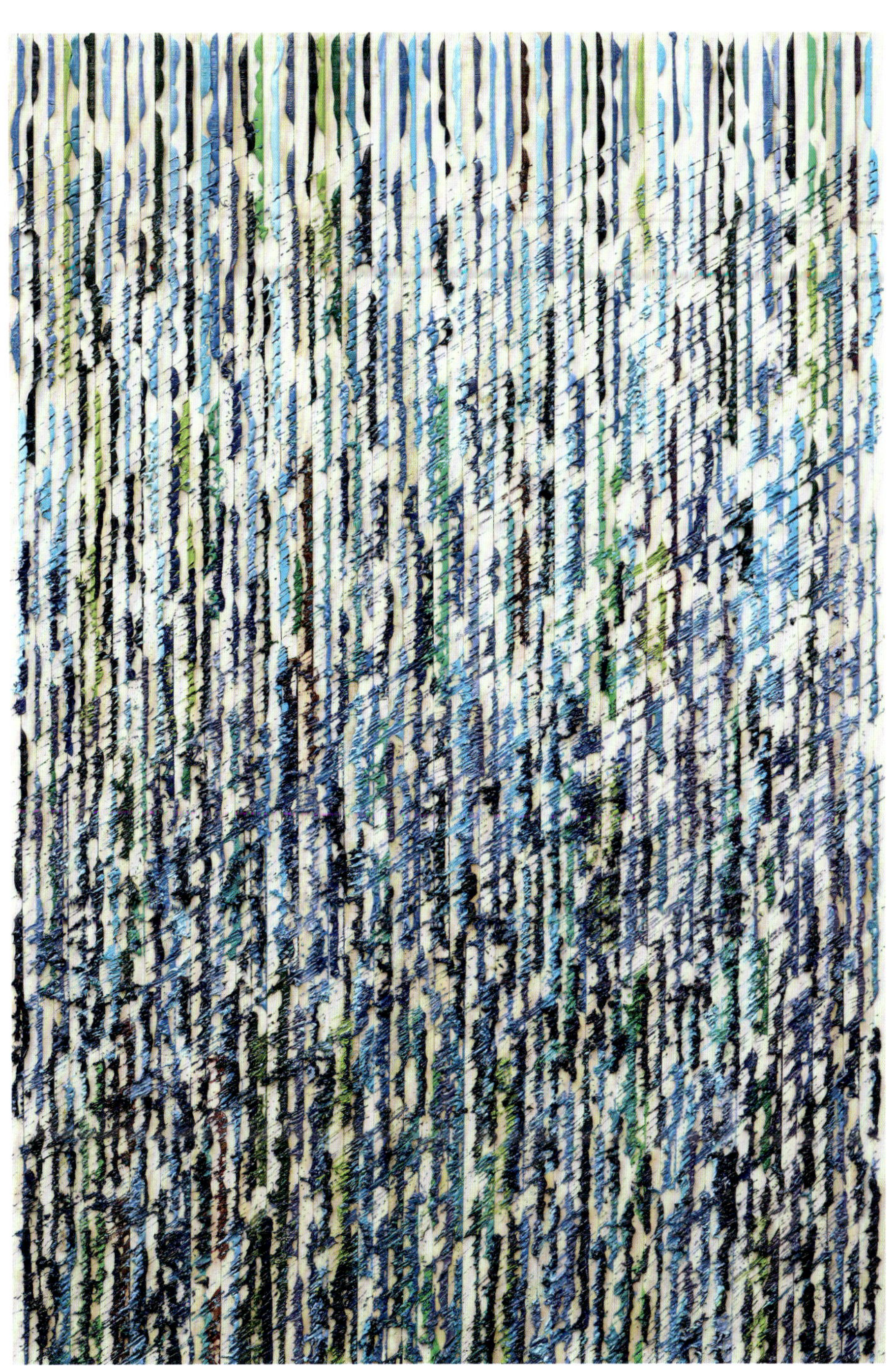

 Post Conjunction 10-(B), 2010. Mixed media, 70 7/8 x 47 1/4 inches (180 x 120 cm)

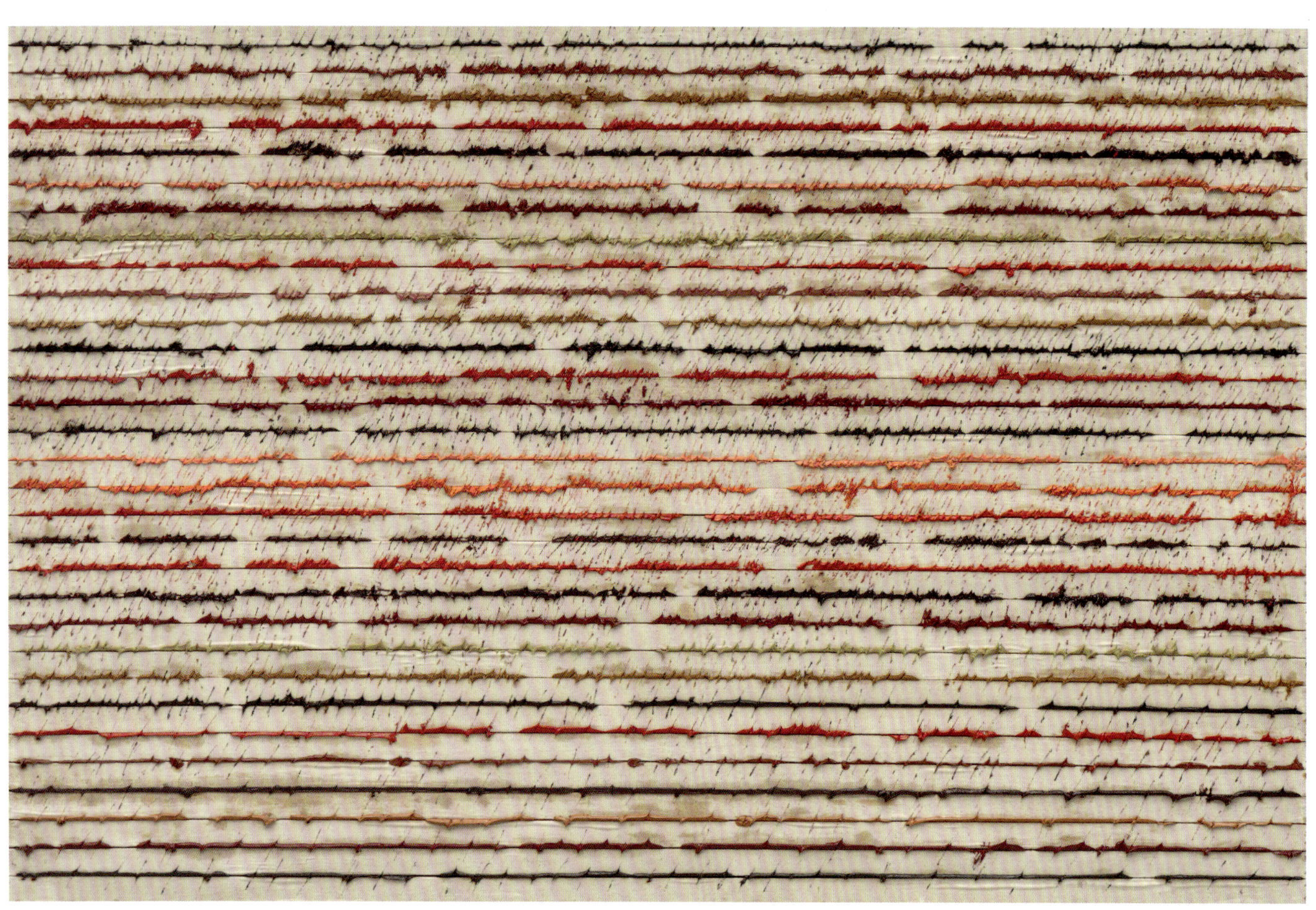

 Post Conjunction 10-31, 2010. Mixed media, 47 1/4 x 70 7/8 inches (120 x 180 cm)

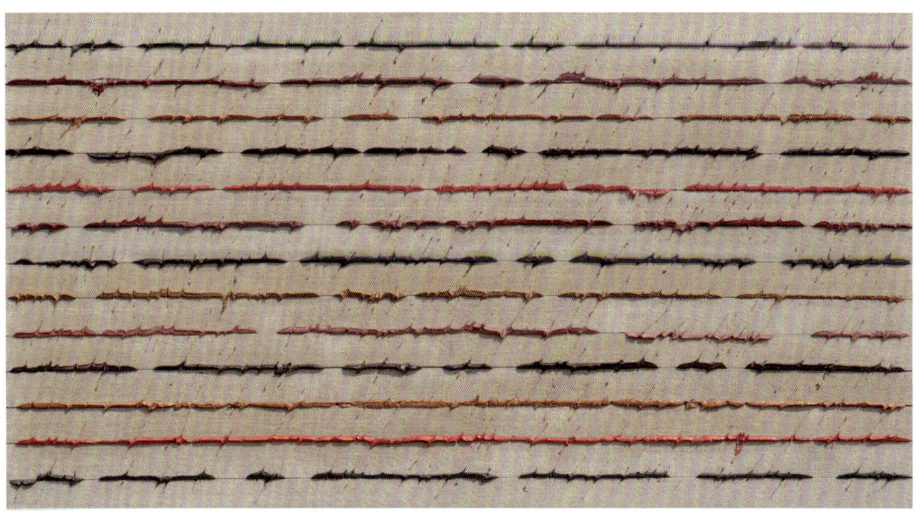

 Post Conjunction 11-42, 2011. Mixed media, 26 x 48 1/8 inches (66 x 122 cm)

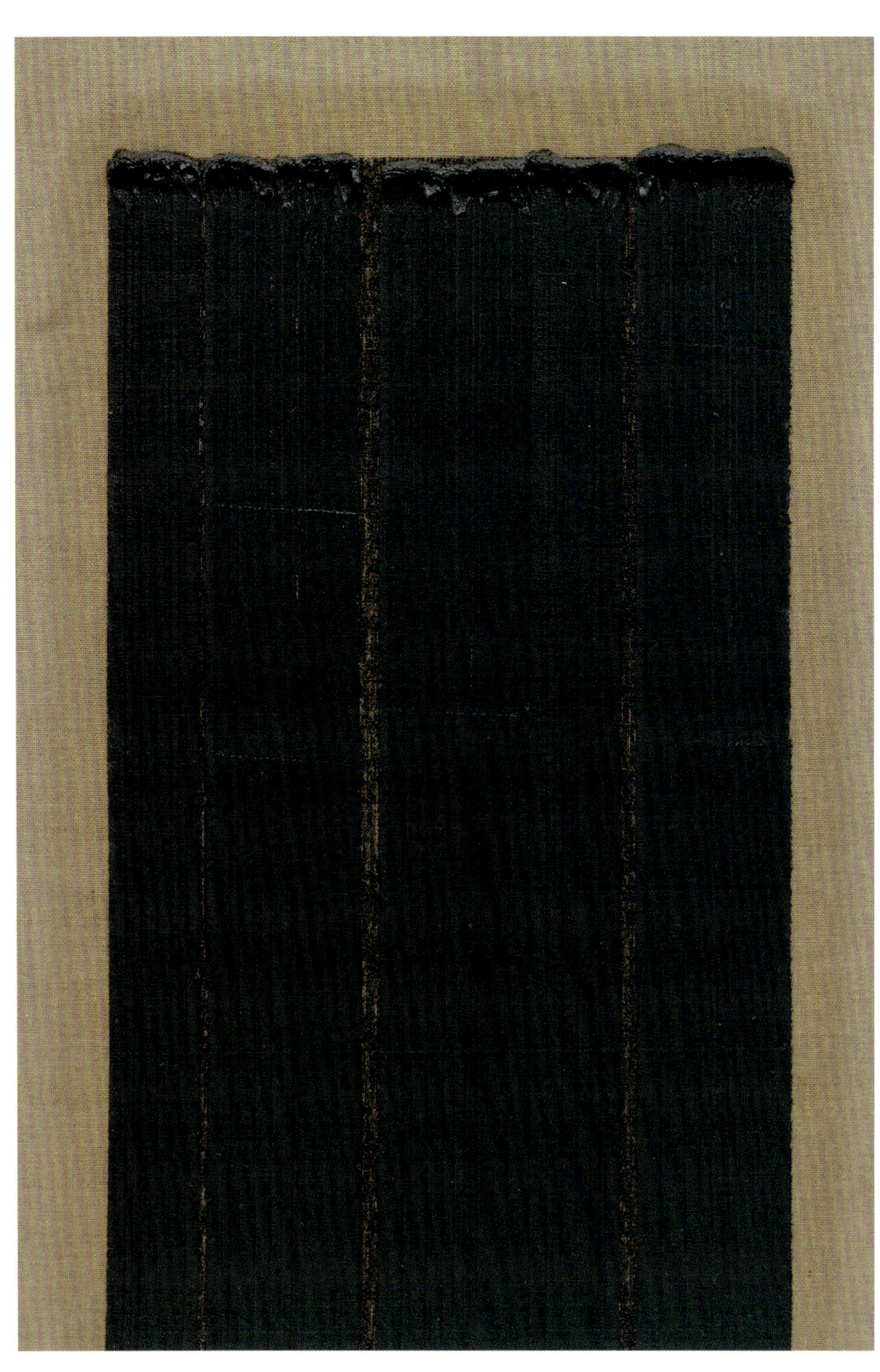

Conjunction 08-121, 2008. Oil on hemp cloth, 70 7/8 x 47 1/4 inches (180 x 120 cm)

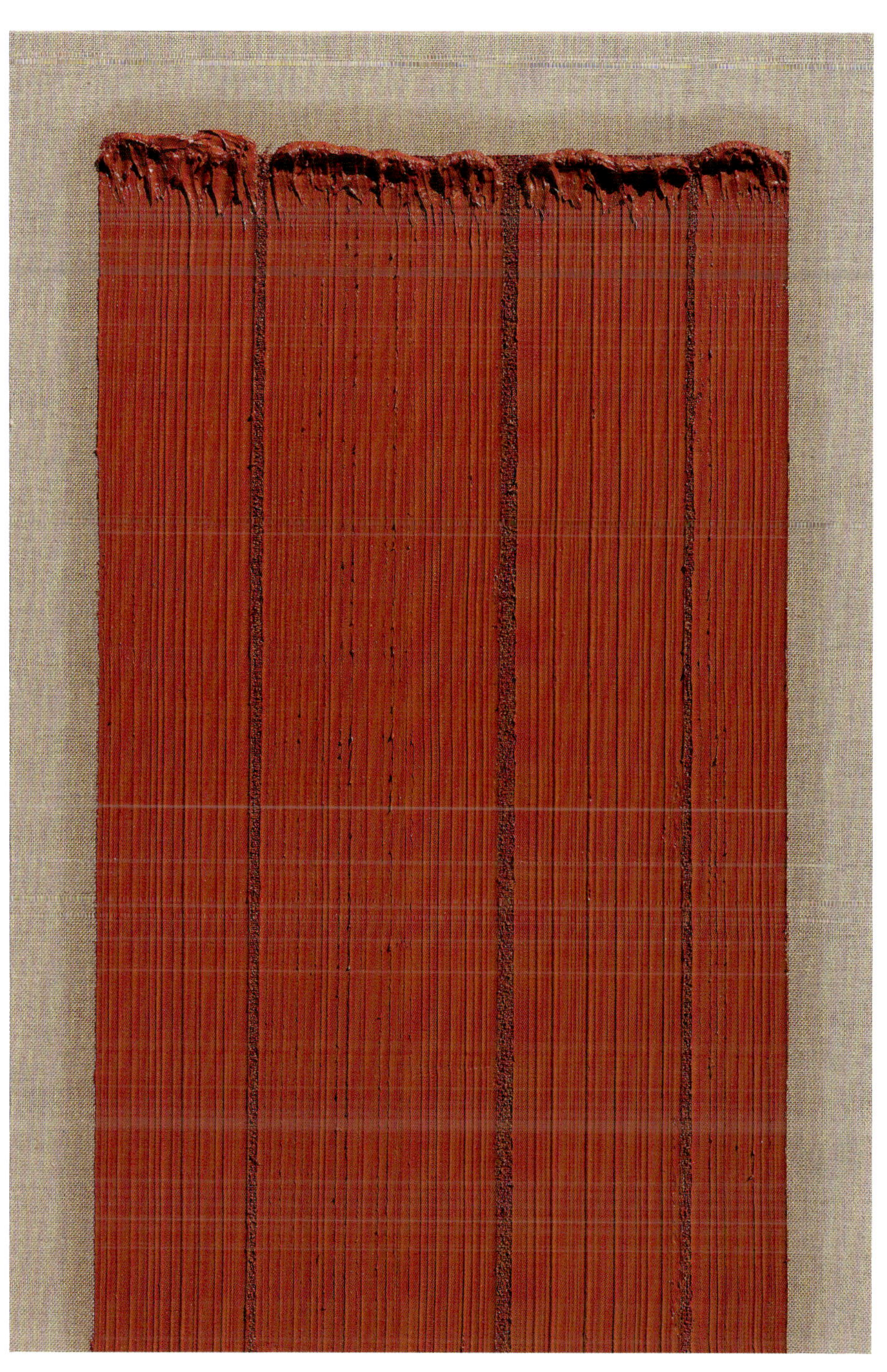

 Conjunction 17-09, 2017. Oil on hemp cloth, 70 7/8 x 47 1/4 inches (180 x 120 cm)

Conjunction 21-73, 2021. Oil on hemp cloth, 70 7/8 x 70 7/8 inches (180 x 180 cm)

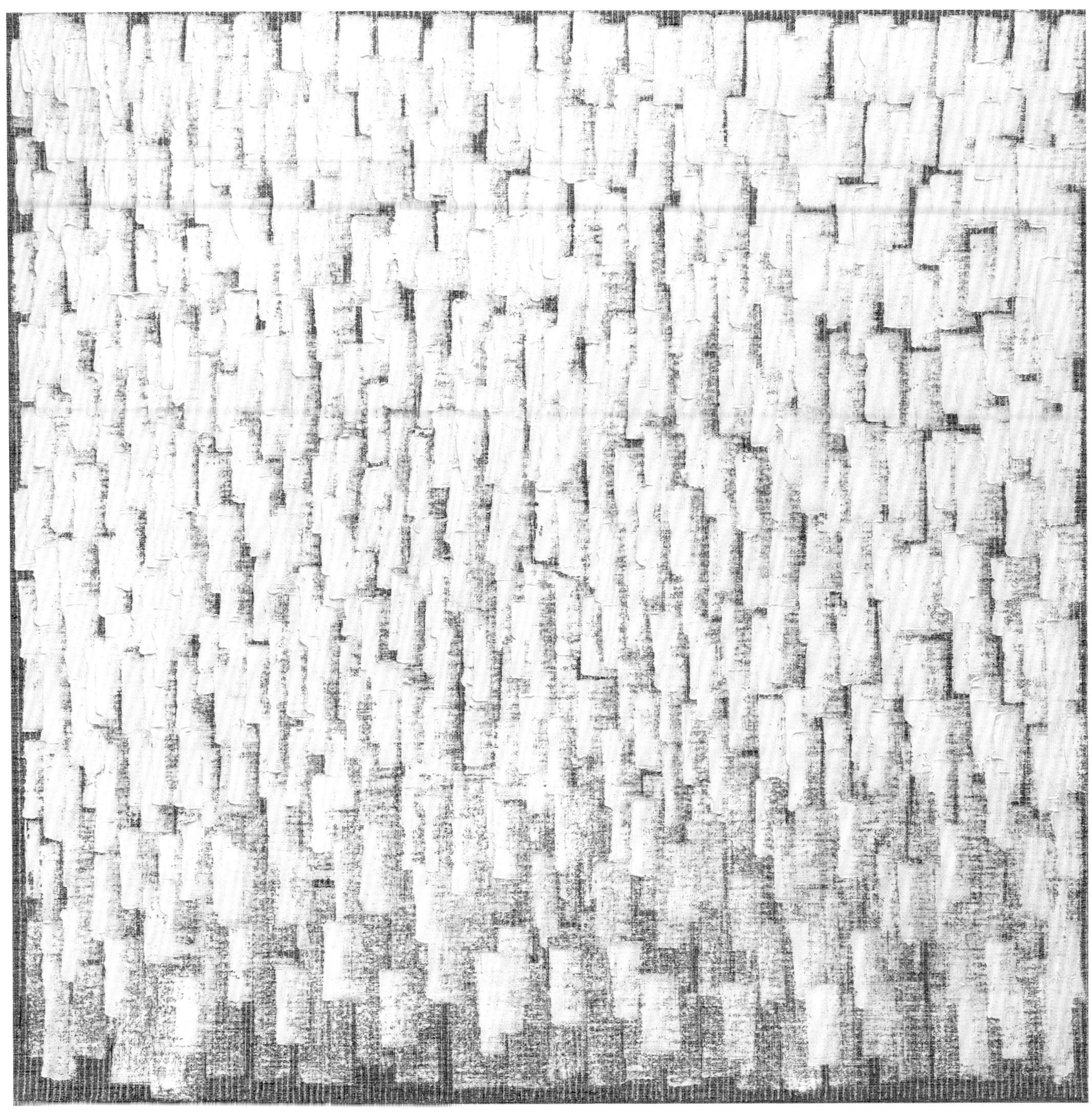

Conjunction 21-74, 2021. Oil on hemp cloth, 70 7/8 x 70 7/8 inches (180 x 180 cm)

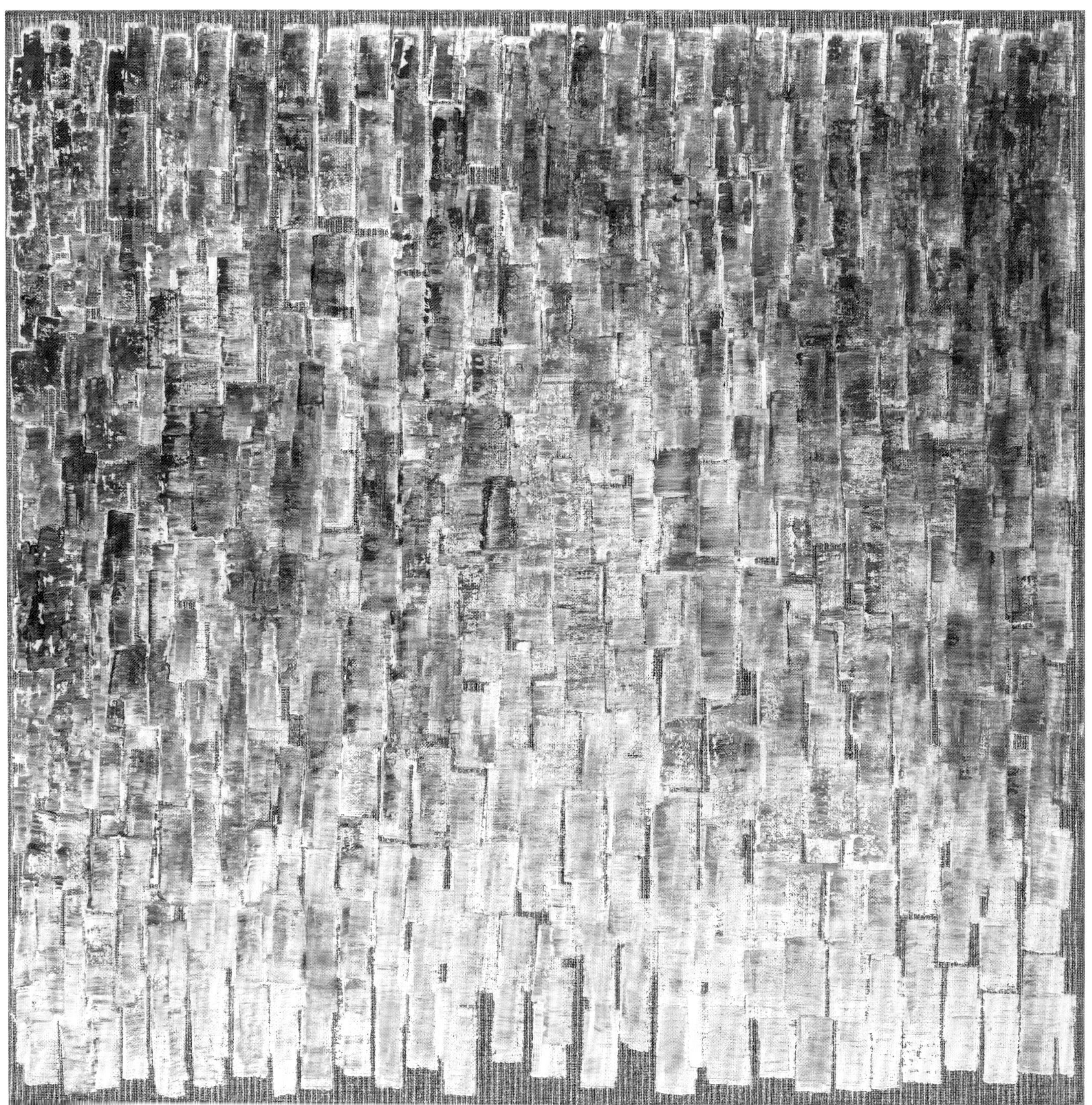

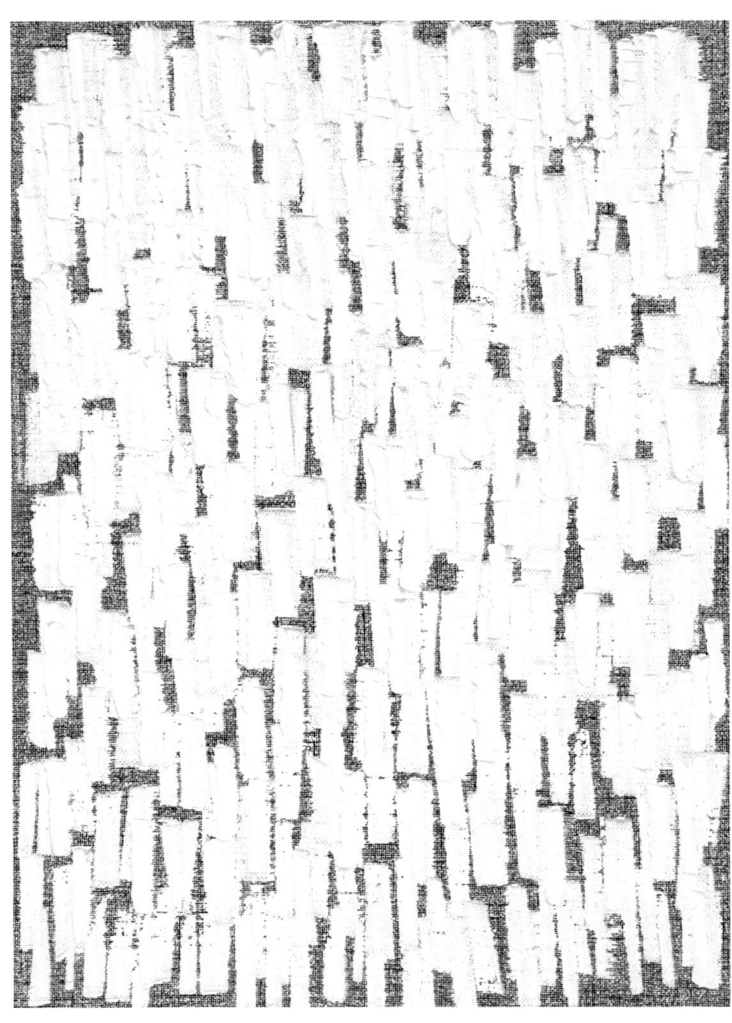

 Conjunction 22-02, 2022. Oil on hemp cloth, 51 1/5 x 38 1/5 inches (130 x 97 cm)

 Conjunction 20-94, 2020. Oil on hemp cloth, 51 1/5 x 38 1/5 inches (130 x 97 cm)

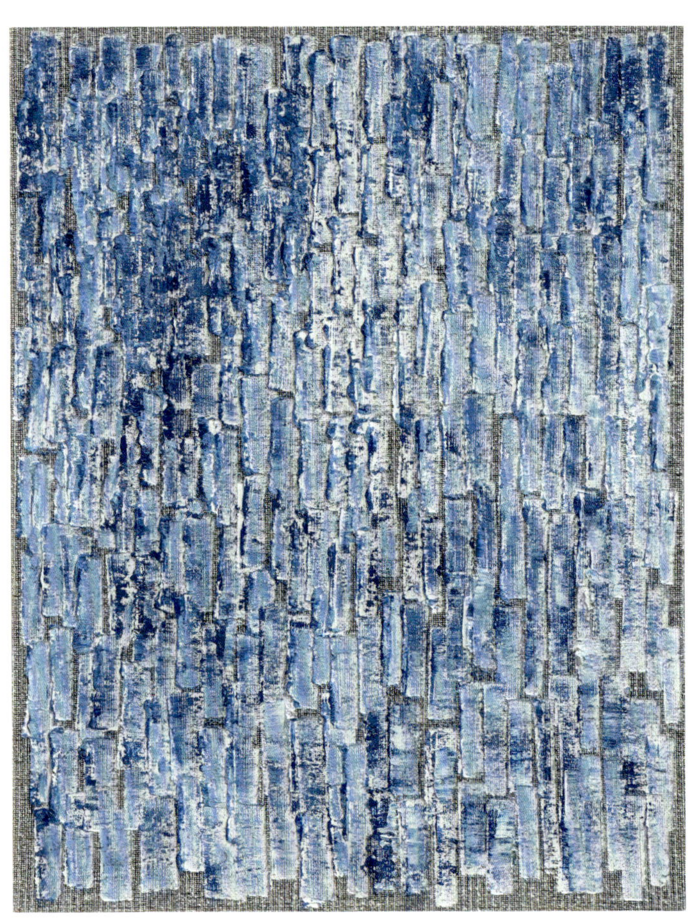

Conjunction 21-32, 2021. Oil on hemp cloth, 46 1/8 x 35 7/8 inches (117 x 91 cm)

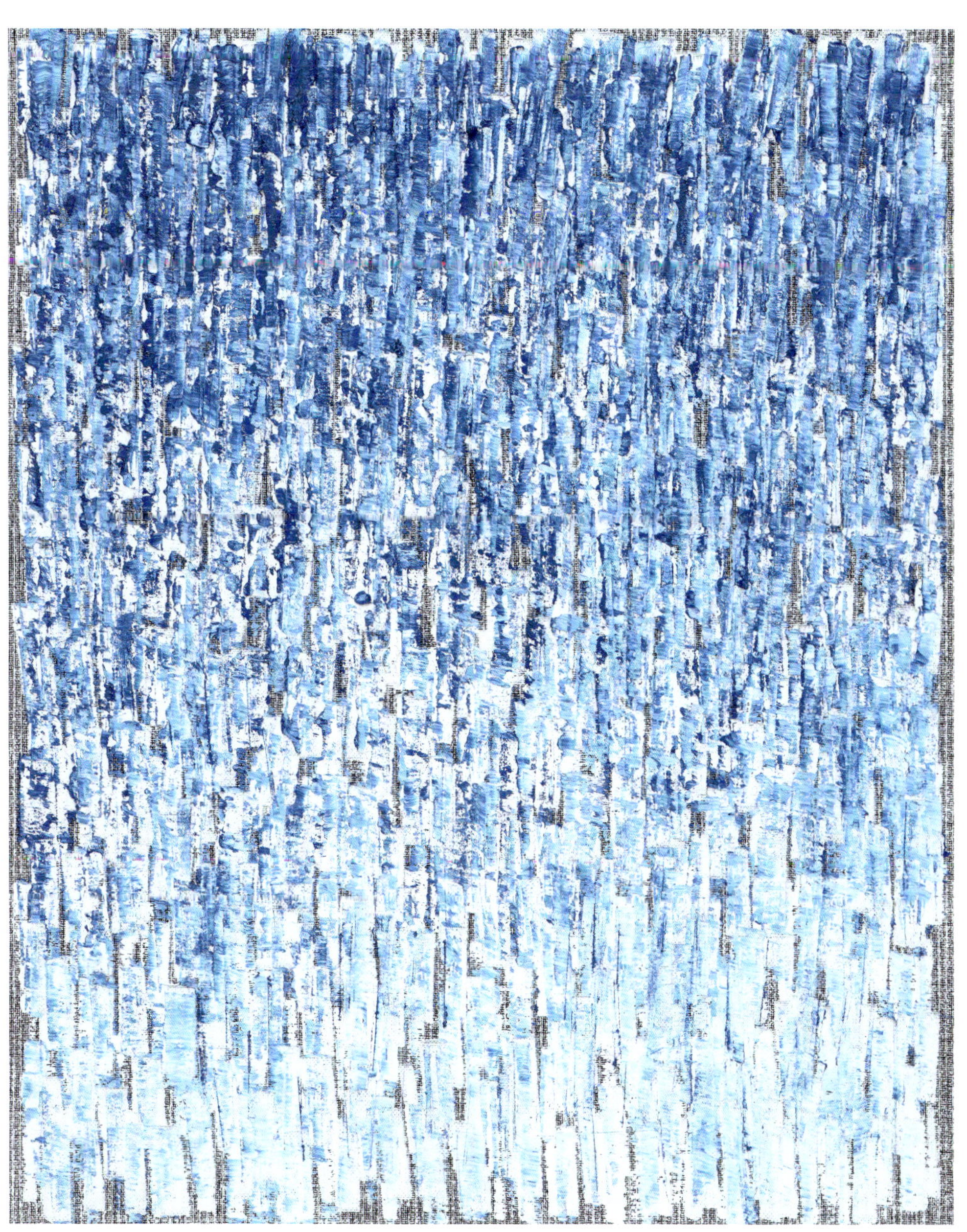

 Conjunction 22-01, 2022. Oil on hemp cloth, 73 3/4 x 51 1/5 inches (162 x 130 cm)

 Conjunction 21-07, 2021. Oil on hemp cloth, 47 1/4 x 47 1/4 inches (120 x 120 cm)

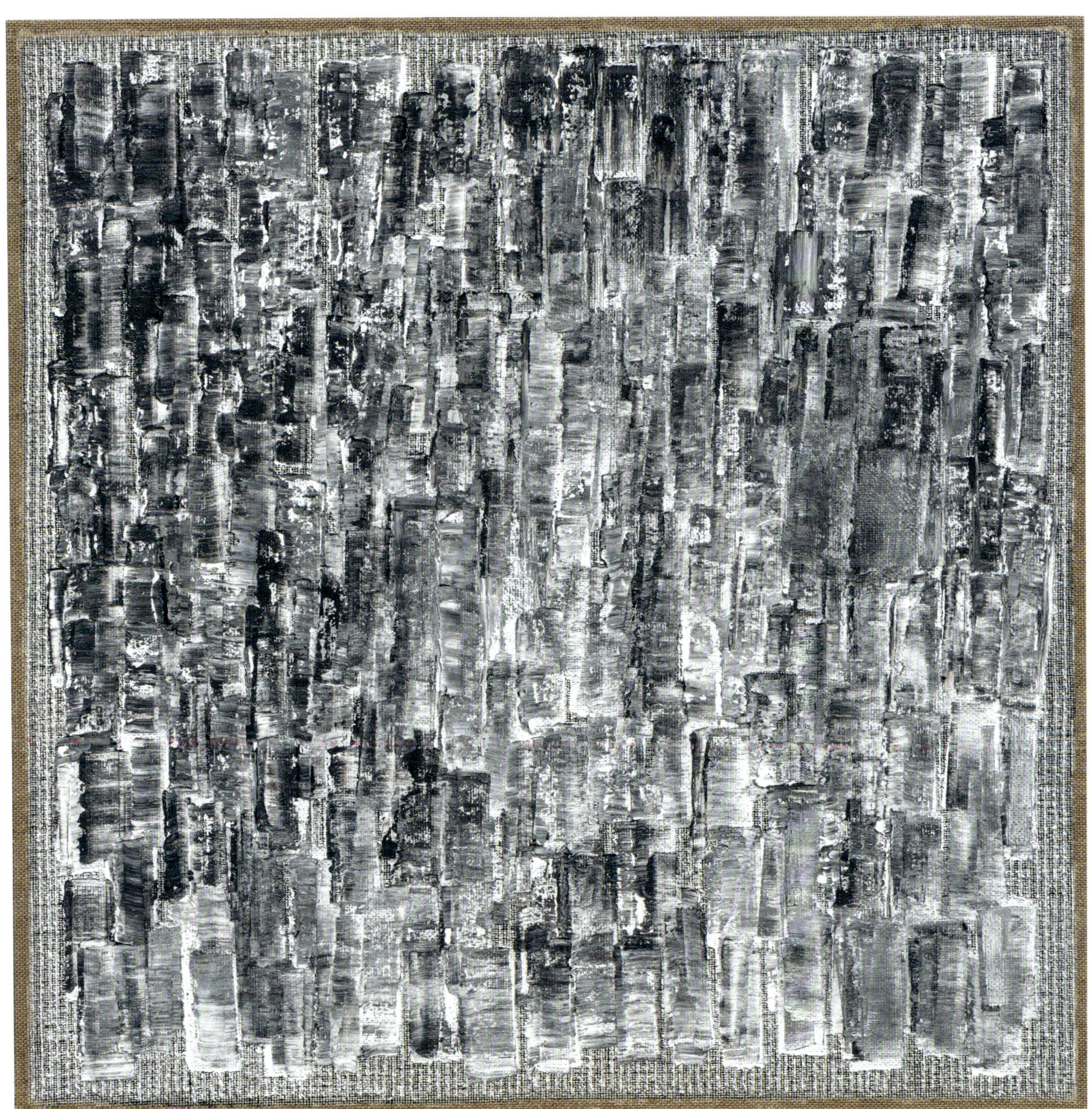

Conjunction 87-8, 1987. Oil on hemp cloth, 31 1/2 x 39 2/5 inches (80 x 100 cm)

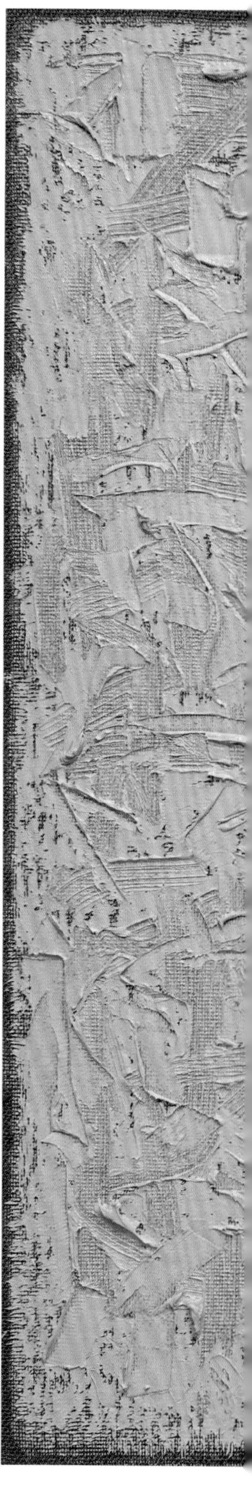

 Conjunction 13-109, 2013. Oil on hemp cloth, 51 x 63 inches (129.5 x 160 cm)

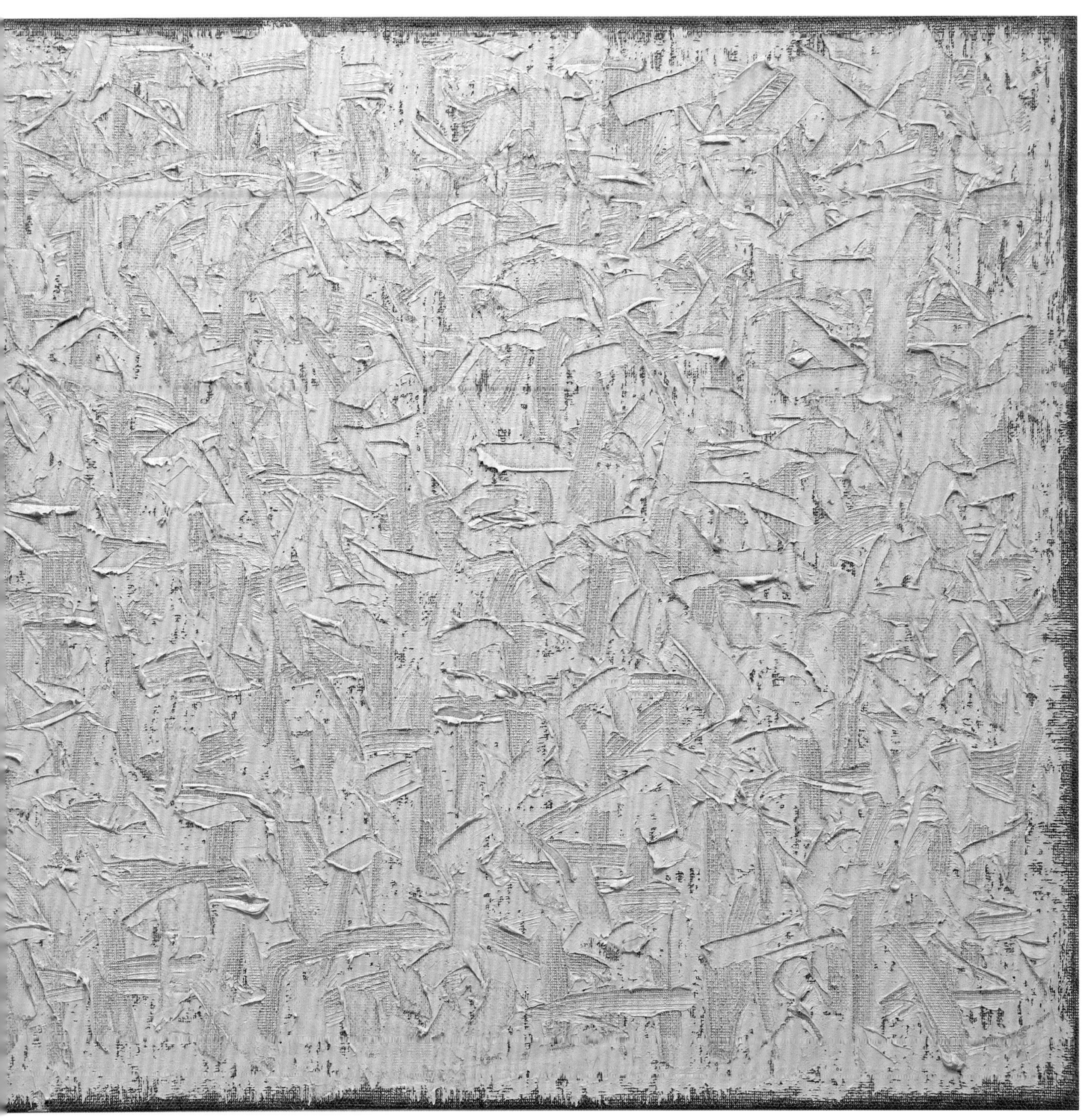

Ha Chong-Hyun in front of *Post Conjunction 11-6*, 2011. Mixed media, 47 1/4 x 72 1/10 inches (120 x 183 cm).

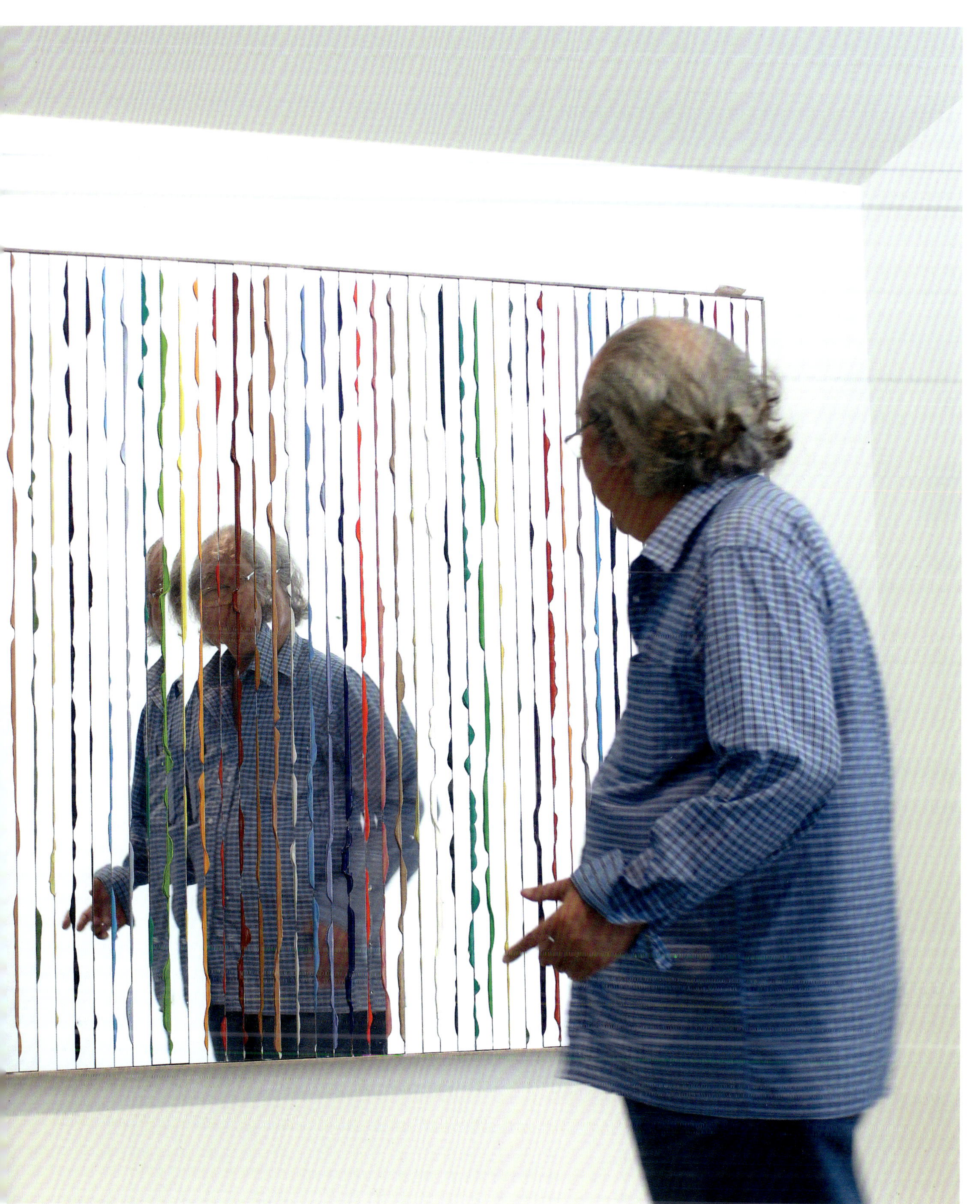

BIOGRAPHY

Ha Chong-Hyun (b. 1935, Sancheong, Korea) graduated from Hongik University in 1959, at a time when a new generation of Korean artists began to absorb the influence of major art movements, including Abstract Expressionism and Informel imported from Europe, the United States, and Japan. The accelerated rate of artistic exchange following the restoration of diplomatic relations with Japan in 1965 led many Dansaekwha artists, including Ha Chong-Hyun, Park Seo-Bo, and Lee Ufan, to participate in the international art fair circuit in the following years. Shortly after Ha first showed the *White Paper on Urban Planning* series in 1967, the Korean AG (Avant-Garde Association) group was established in Seoul by twelve artists and critics associated with Hongik University, followed by the publication of the inaugural issue of the journal *AG* in 1969. As a member and chairman of the AG group from 1969 to 1974, Ha participated in all four AG exhibitions and published "Entering the Year of 1970 in Korean Art" in the second issue of *AG*.

Ha began his signature *Conjunction* series in 1974 and used the color white exclusively until 1977. *Conjunction* refers to the physical connection between the two most important elements of Ha's practice, his methods and his materials, and how the two are intertwined, or conjoined. The burlap he began to substitute for the more traditional canvas after the Korean War allowed him to approach each painting from the reverse side, pushing thick paint through the loose weave. Ha's interest in the simple muted tones of hemp stems from his work in the 1970s, when he bravely explored non-traditional materials, including plaster, newspaper, barbed wire, and the burlap that was used to transport food aid from the United States following the Korean War. Burlap was found throughout Korea and was immediately recognizable, and Ha's choice of this ordinary but politically charged material, as well as other cast-off items from the war, set the stage for a radical confrontation between traditional painting and his politicized milieu. The seminal *Five Korean Artists, Five Kinds of White* exhibition in 1975, widely regarded as the beginning of the Dansaekwha movement, led to the formation of the École de Seoul by Park Seo-Bo. Ha shared the Dansaekwha group's reconsideration of the medium of painting and became affiliated with it. Ha introduced shades of khaki and golden brown and eventually incorporated a dark blue coloration into his *Conjunction* paintings by the early 1980s, the height of the Minjung art movement. Since 2010, Ha has been developing his *Post Conjunction* series.

In 1993, Ha exhibited in *12 Contemporary Artists from Korea*, a collateral exhibition that was part of the forty-fifth Venice Biennale. Awarded an honorary doctorate degree by his alma mater, Hongik University, Ha also taught there as a lecturer from 1962 to 1966 and was appointed professor of the College of Fine Arts from 1967 to 2001. He served as the dean of the College of Fine Arts from 1990 to 1994, and he is currently emeritus professor. From 2001 to 2006, Ha was the director of the Seoul Museum of Art. Ha's undeniable importance as a central figure for modern Korean art has placed his work in the permanent collections of the Solomon R. Guggenheim Museum in New York; Centre Pompidou in Paris; Art Institute of Chicago; M+ in Hong Kong; Tokyo Metropolitan Art Museum; Hiroshima City Museum of Contemporary Art; Leeum, Samsung Museum of Art in Seoul; and Korea's National Museum of Modern and Contemporary Art.

EXHIBITIONS AND COLLECTIONS

HA CHONG-HYUN

1935
Born in Sancheong, Korea

1959
Graduated from the Department of Painting, Hongik University, Seoul, Korea

SELECTED SOLO EXHIBITIONS

2022 (forthcoming) Palazzetto Tito, Venice, Italy
Ha Chong-Hyun, Kukje Gallery, Seoul, Korea
2021 *Ha Chong-Hyun: Return to Color*, Tina Kim Gallery, New York, US
2020 Almine Rech Gallery, London, UK
Daejeon Museum of Art, Korea
2019 Kukje Gallery, Busan, Korea
Cardi Gallery, Milan, Italy
Blum & Poe, Tokyo, Japan
2018 *Ha Chong-Hyun: Conjunction*, Tina Kim Gallery, New York, US
2017 Almine Rech Gallery, London, UK
Almine Rech Gallery, Paris, France
2016 Blum & Poe, Los Angeles, US
2015 Tina Kim Gallery, New York, US
Kukje Gallery, Seoul, Korea
2014 Blum & Poe, New York, US
2012 National Museum of Modern and Contemporary Art, Gwacheon, Korea
2010 Severance Art Space, Seoul, Korea
2009 Seok Gallery, Daegu, Korea
Bluedot M Gallery, Changwon, Korea
Rother Winter Gallery, Wiesbaden, Germany
2008 Gana Art Center, Seoul, Korea
2004 Gyeongnam Art Museum, Changwon, Korea
Gallery Bijutsu Sekai, Tokyo, Japan
2003 Mudima Foundation for Contemporary Art, Milan, Italy
2002 Busan Museum of Art, Korea
Gallery Bijutsu Sekai, Tokyo, Japan
2001 Kamakura Gallery, Tokyo, Japan,
Chosunilbo Museum of Art, Seoul, Korea
2000 Hongik University Museum, Seoul, Korea
1999 Espace Paul Ricard, Paris, France
1997 Samtuh Gallery, Seoul, Korea
Kamakura Gallery, Tokyo, Japan
1996 Biever-Risch Galerie, Luxembourg, Luxembourg
1995 Hanlim Gallery, Daejeon, Korea
1994 Wassermann Gallery, Munich, Germany
Kamakura Gallery, Tokyo, Japan
1992 Art Center Nabi, Seoul, Korea
1990 Kamakura Gallery, Tokyo, Japan
1985 Kamakura Gallery, Tokyo, Japan
1984 Gallery Hyundai, Seoul, Korea
1979 Muramatsu Gallery, Tokyo, Japan

EXHIBITIONS AND COLLECTIONS

1977 Space Gallery, Seoul, Korea
1975 Moonhun Gallery, Seoul, Korea
1974 Myung-Dong Gallery, Seoul, Korea
1972 Gin Gallery, Tokyo, Japan

SELECTED GROUP EXHIBITIONS

2021 Rho Gallery, Seoul, Korea
Jamunbak Museum Project: Part I, Gana Art Center, Seoul, Korea
Resonance, Horim Museum, Seoul, Korea
2020 *Tina Kim Gallery Presents: Art Without Borders*, Tina Kim Gallery, New York, US
2019 *War Within, War Without, Collection 1940s–1970s*, Museum of Modern Art, New York, US
Awakenings: Art in Society in Asia 1960s–1990s, National Museum of Modern and Contemporary Art, Gwacheon, Korea
Abstraction(s), Song Art Museum, Beijing, China
Landlord Colors: On Art, Economy, and Materiality, Cranbrook Art Museum, Bloomfield Hills, Michigan, US
2018 *Korean Abstract Art: Kim Whanki and Dansaekhwa*, Powerlong Museum, Shanghai, China
Renegades in Resistance and Challenge, Daegu Art Museum, Korea
Topologies, curated by Mika Yoshitake, The Warehouse, Dallas, US
2017 *Rhythm in Monochrome: Korean Abstract Painting,* Tokyo Opera City Art Gallery, Japan
The Ascetic Path: Korean Dansaekhwa, Erarta Museum, Saint Petersburg, Russia
Arts of Korea, Brooklyn Museum, US
Asian Diva: The Muse and the Monster, Seoul Museum of Art, Korea
Looking into Korean Art, Part 2: Dansaekhwa, Museum SAN, Wonju, Korea
Thinking Out Loud: Notes for an Evolving Collection, Warehouse, Rachofsky Collection, Dallas, US
2016 *Dansaekhwa and Minimalism*, Blum & Poe, New York and Los Angeles, US
KM 9346: Korea-Morbihan 9,346km, Domaine de Kerguéhennec, Bignan, France
30 Years 1986–2016: As the Moon Waxes and Wanes, National Museum of Modern and Contemporary Art, Gwacheon, Korea
When Process Becomes Form: Dansaekhwa and Korean Abstraction, Villa Empain–Boghossian Foundation, Brussels, Belgium
New Beginnings: Between Gesture and Geometry, Athens, Greece
Hybridizing Earth/Discussing Multitude, Busan Biennale, Korea
2015 *Dansaekhwa*, Venice Biennale, Italy
Avant Garde Asia: Lines of Korean Masters, Sotheby's Hong Kong Gallery, Hong Kong, China
Bold Abstractions: Selections from the DMA Collection 1966–1976, Dallas Museum of Art, US
PROPORTIO, Palazzo Fortuny, Italy
45th Anniversary of Gallery Hyundai: Korean Abstract Painting, Gallery Hyundai, Seoul, Korea
Gallery Roh, Seoul, Korea

EXHIBITIONS AND COLLECTIONS

2014 *The Art of Dansaekhwa*, Kukje Gallery, Seoul, Korea
From All Sides: Tansaekhwa on Abstraction, Blum & Poe, Los Angeles, US
Unconstraint Creation, Hakgojae Gallery, Shanghai, China
Overcoming the Modern: Dansaekhwa, The Korean Monochrome Movement, Alexander Gray Associates, New York, US
Empty Fullness: Materiality and Spirituality in Contemporary Korean Art, Korean Cultural Center, Beijing, China; traveled to SPSI Art Museum, Shanghai, China; Koreanisches Kulturzentrum, Berlin, Germany; National Museum of Indonesia, Jakarta, Indonesia

2012 *Dansaekhwa: Korean Monochrome Painting*, National Museum of Modern and Contemporary Art, Gwacheon, Korea

2011 *Qi Is Full*, Daegu Art Museum, Korea
The Spectrum of Contemporary Korean Art, Kaohsiung Museum of Fine Arts, Taiwan

2010 *Korean Avant-Garde Drawing: 1970–2000*, Seoul Olympic Museum of Art, Korea

2009 *Bong Whang 137*, Sunshine International Art Museum, Beijing, China
Monochrome Art in Korea, Wellside Gallery, Shanghai, China

2008 Fifth Busan Biennale, Korea
Korean Abstract Art 1958–2008, Seoul Museum of Art, Korea
The Color of Nature: Monochrome Art in Korea, Pyo Gallery, Seoul, Korea

2007 *Contemplation on a Space*, Gana Art Center, Busan, Korea
Abstract Art: Amusement on the Border, Seoul Museum of Art, Korea

2004 *Korean Contemporary Paintings: Past and Now*, Seoul Museum of Art, Korea

2003 *The Seoul Art Exhibition*, Seoul Museum of Art, Korea

2002 *Age of Philosophy and Aesthetics*, National Museum of Modern and Contemporary Art, Gwacheon, Korea

2001 *Development of Korean Contemporary Art*, National Museum of Modern and Contemporary Art, Gwacheon, Korea

2000 *Postwar Abstract Art in Korea and West: Passion and Expression*, Ho-Am Art Museum, Seoul, Korea
The Facets of Korean and Japanese Contemporary Art, Gwangju Biennale, Korea
Passage to the New Millennium, National Museum of Modern and Contemporary Art, Gwacheon, Korea
Plane as Spirits, Busan Museum of Art, Korea
The Horizon of a New Millennium, Gallery Hyundai, Seoul, Korea

1998 *Les peintres du silence—Huit maitres contemporains*, Musée Montbeliard, France
PICAF, Busan Museum of Art, Korea

1996 *Korean Monochrome Paintings of the 1970s*, Gallery Hyundai, Seoul, Korea

1995 *The Tiger's Tail: 15 Korean Contemporary Artists for Venice 95*, Palazzo Vendramin, Venice, Italy
Seoul International Painting Exhibition, National Museum of Modern and Contemporary Art, Gwacheon, Korea
Korean Contemporary Paintings, Hanlim Gallery, Daejeon, Korea
Contemporary Korean Paintings, Paris City Museum, France
Nature of Korea, Park Ryu Sook Gallery, Seoul, Korea

1993 *12 Contemporary Artists from Korea*, Miyagi Museum, Sendai, Japan; Venice Biennale, Italy
Korean Contemporary Art, Total Museum of Contemporary Art, Seoul, Korea

1992 *Flows from the Far East: Recent Korean Art Scene*, Concourse Gallery, Barbican Centre, London, UK

1991 *Korean Contemporary Paintings*, Museum of Contemporary Art, Zagreb, Croatia; traveled to Cankarjev dom, Ljubljana, Slovenia; Collegium Artisticum, Sarajevo, Bosnia; Museum of Contemporary Art, Belgrade, Serbia

1990 *Korean Art Today*, Seoul Arts Center, Korea

1989 *Hiroshima*, Hiroshima City Museum of Contemporary Art, Japan

1988 *The 4 Korean Artists*, Tokyo Gallery, Japan

The 24th Olympic International Modern Arts Exhibition, National Museum of Modern and Contemporary Art, Gwacheon, Korea

1987 *The 31st Toyama International Arts Exhibition*, Toyama, Japan

4 Korean Contemporary Artists, Laboratory Gallery, Sapporo, Japan

1986 *Korean Arts Yesterday and Today*, National Museum of Modern and Contemporary Art, Gwacheon, Korea

Asian Contemporary Arts, National Museum of Modern and Contemporary Art, Gwacheon, Korea

1985 *The 3rd Human Documents 1984–1985*, Tokyo Gallery, Japan

70 Years of Korean Western Painting, Ho-Am Art Museum, Seoul, Korea

Modern Art from the Past 40 Years, National Museum of Modern and Contemporary Art, Seoul, Korea

1984 *Contemporary Korean Art: The Late 1970s—A Situation*, Korean Culture and Arts Foundation Art Center, Seoul, Korea

Korean Contemporary Art '84, Taipei Fine Arts Museum, Taiwan

Korean Arts of the 1960s, Walker Hill Museum, Seoul, Korea

Korean Contemporary Art in the 1960s, Duson Gallery, Seoul, Korea

1983 *Korean Contemporary Arts Exhibition of the 1970s Exhibition*, Tokyo Metropolitan Art Museum; traveled to Fukuoka Art Museum, Japan; National Museum of Art, Osaka, Japan; Hokkaido Museum of Modern Art, Sapporo, Japan; and Tochigi Prefectural Museum of Fine Arts, Japan

Exchange Exhibition of Print and Drawing Between Seoul and San Francisco, Seoul & World Print Council, San Francisco, and Korean Cultural Service, Los Angeles, US

Korea: New Paper Works, Spring Gallery, Taipei, Taiwan

1982—1983

The Art of Contemporary Paper: Korea and Japan, National Museum of Modern and Contemporary Art, Deoksugung, Korea; Kyoto Municipal Museum of Art, Japan; Museum of Modern Art Saitama, Japan; Kumamoto International Folk Craft Museum, Japan

1981 *Drawing '81*, National Museum of Modern and Contemporary Art, Seoul, Korea

Works on Paper: Korean Contemporary Drawings, Dongsanbang Gallery, Seoul, Korea, and Art Core Gallery, Los Angeles, US

Drawings by Korean Artists, Brooklyn Museum, US

Contemporary Asian Arts, Fukuoka Art Museum, Japan

1978 2ème Rencontres Internationales d'art Contemporain, Galeries Nationales du Grand Palais, Paris, France

The Trend for the Past 20 Years in Korean Contemporary Art, National Museum of Modern and Contemporary Art, Seoul, Korea

1977 13th São Paulo Bienal, Brazil

Korean Contemporary Art, National Museum of History, Taipei, Taiwan

1975 3rd Triennale—India, New Delhi, India

4th Avant Garde Exhibition, National Museum of Modern and Contemporary Art, Seoul, Korea

1974 6th Cagnes International Painting Festival, France
1st Seoul Biennale, Korea

1973 *Korean Contemporary Art 1957–1972: Formative and Informative*, Myung-Dong Gallery, Seoul, Korea
13 Contemporary Artists, Signum Gallery, Tokyo, Japan
Exhibition of 100 Modern Korean Painters, National Museum of Modern and Contemporary Art, Deoksugung, Korea

1972 *3rd Avant Garde Exhibition*, National Museum of Modern and Contemporary Art, Seoul, Korea

1969—1972
Korean Contemporary Painting Exhibition: toured Japan, India, Pakistan, and Nepal

1971 *2nd Avant Garde Exhibition: Reality and Realization*, National Museum of Modern and Contemporary Art, Seoul, Korea
7th Biennale de Paris, France

1970 *1st Avant Garde Exhibition*, Korean Information Center Gallery, Seoul, Korea
7th Tokyo Print Biennale, National Museum of Modern Art, Japan
6 Korean Contemporary Artists, Tokiwa Gallery, Tokyo, Japan

1960—1969
The Contemporary Art Exhibit, National Museum of Modern and Contemporary Art, Seoul, Korea

1969 *11 Young Artists from Korea*, Solidaridad Gallery, Manila, Philippines

1968 Korean Contemporary Painting Exhibition, Tokyo Metropolitan Art Museum, Japan

1967 9th São Paulo Bienal, Brazil

1965 4th Biennale de Paris, France
4th Cultural Freedom Invitational Exhibition, Yechong Gallery, Seoul, Korea

1961 2nd Paris Youth Biennale, France

SELECTED MUSEUMS AND PUBLIC COLLECTIONS

Art and Culture Foundation of Ilshin, Seoul, Korea
Art Institute of Chicago, US
Ewha Womans University Museum, Seoul, Korea
Fukuoka Art Museum, Japan
George Economou Collection, Athens, Greece
Gwangju Museum of Art, Gwangju, Korea
Gyeonggi Museum of Modern Art, Ansan, Korea
Hiroshima City Museum of Contemporary Art, Japan
Ho-Am Art Museum, Yongin, Korea
Hongik University Museum, Seoul, Korea
Hwajeong Museum, Seoul, Korea
Leeum, Samsung Museum of Art, Seoul, Korea
M+, Hong Kong, China
Mie Prefectural Art Museum, Japan
Miyagi Museum of Art, Japan
Museum of Modern Art, New York, US
Museum of Modern Art, Toyama, Japan

EXHIBITIONS AND COLLECTIONS

Museum Voorlinden, Wassenaar, Netherlands
National Museum of Modern and Contemporary Art, Korea
OCT Boxes Art Museum, Guangdong Province, China
Posco Art Museum, Seoul, Korea
Rachofsky Collection, Dallas, US
Seoul Museum of Art, Korea
Seoul Olympic Museum of Art, Korea
Solomon R. Guggenheim Museum, New York, US
Shimonoseki City Art Museum, Japan
Tokyo Metropolitan Art Museum, Japan

AUTHOR BIOGRAPHIES

SUNJUNG KIM is the artistic director of the Art Sonje Center and the founder and artistic director of the REAL DMZ PROJECT. Previously she was chief curator and deputy director (1993–2004) and then director (2016–17) of the Art Sonje Center, where she curated numerous exhibitions, including solo exhibitions of Lee Bul (1998, 2012), Haegue Yang (2010), Abraham Cruzvillegas (2015), Francis Alÿs (2018), and Chen Chieh-Jen (2021). She was also the commissioner of the Korean pavilion for the 51st Venice Biennale in 2005, the artistic director of Platform Seoul (2006–10), the artistic director of Media City Seoul (2010), a co-artistic director of the 2012 Gwangju Biennale, the artistic director of the ACC Archive & Research at the Asia Culture Center (2014–15), and the president of the Gwangju Biennale Foundation (2017–21).

CLARA KIM is the Daskalopoulos Senior Curator of International Art at Tate Modern. At Tate, she oversees the acquisition, collection, and interpretation of modern and contemporary art from Africa, Asia, and the Middle East, while curating exhibitions and displays including *Steve McQueen* (2020), *A Year in Art: 1973* (2019–20), *Kara Walker: Fons Americanus* (2019), and *Christian Marclay: The Clock* (2018–19).

YEON SHIM CHUNG is a professor in the department of art history and theory at Hongik University in Seoul, South Korea. She received her Ph.D. in art history at the Institute of Fine Arts, New York University. Before earning tenure at Hongik, Dr. Chung was an assistant professor in the art history department at FIT/SUNY in New York City and a researcher for the exhibition *The Worlds of Nam June Paik* at the Solomon R. Guggenheim Museum, New York, in 1999. She also co-curated *Faultlines* (2018 Gwangju Biennale) and the 2014 Gwangju Biennale Special Exhibition. In 2013, Chung compiled a critical anthology of Lee Yil, a major proponent of Dansaekhwa in postwar Korean art (Mijinsa, 2013; English translation published by Les Presses du Réel, 2018). She authored several articles on Dansaekhwa at *M+ Matters* (Hong Kong), and monographs on Lee Bul, Nam June Paik, Park Hyun-Ki, and Korean experimental avant-garde artists. She co-authored and co-edited *Korean Art from 1953: Collision, Innovation, Interaction* (London: Phaidon, 2020). Chung was a Fulbright fellow and visiting research professor at IFA/NYU in 2018–19.

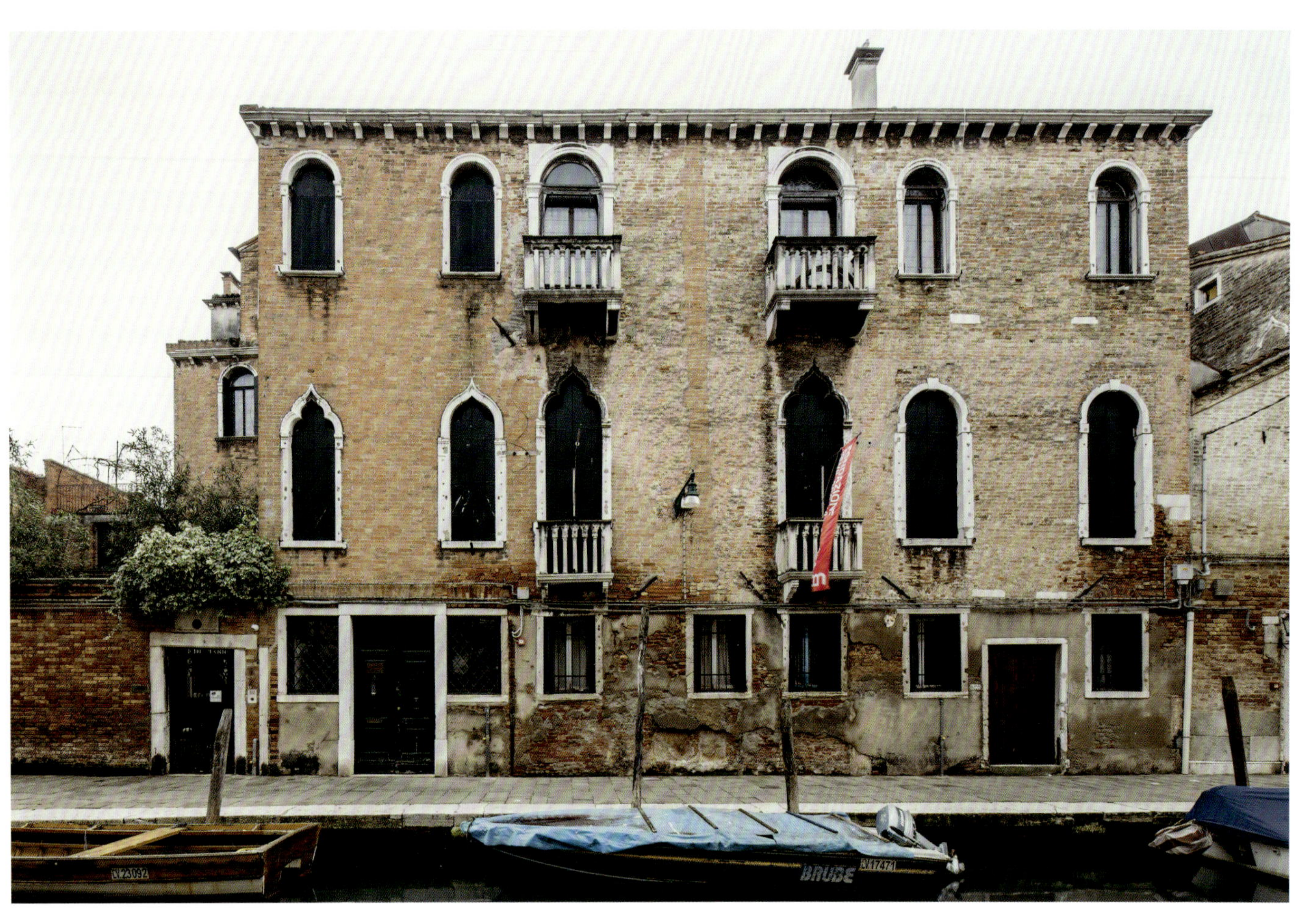

 Palazzetto Tito, Dorsoduro, Venice.

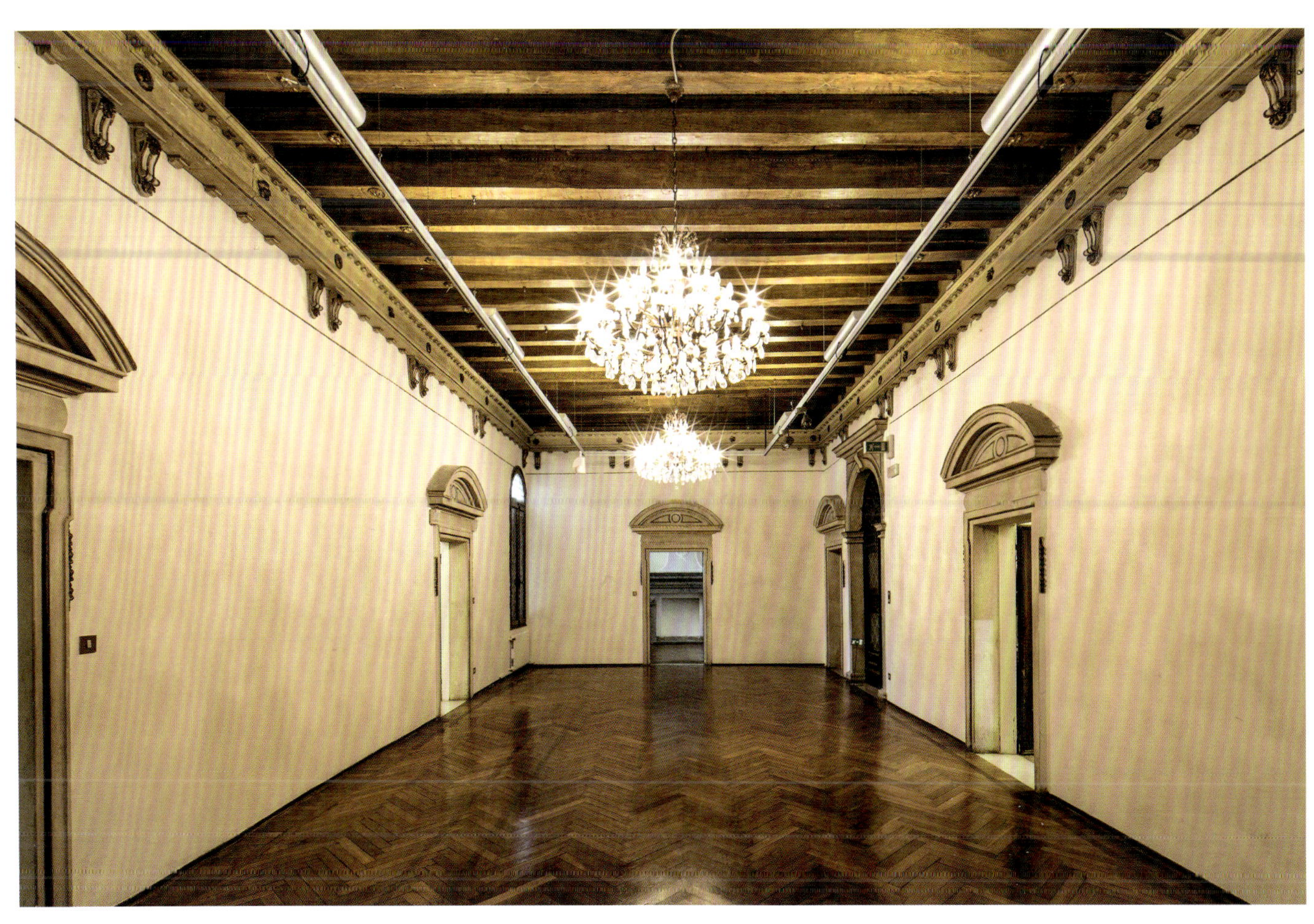

123 Interior of Palazzetto Tito, Venice.

PHOTOGRAPHY CREDITS

Fabrice Seixas: 4–5, 25. Science History Images/Alamy: 7 fig. 1. Courtesy of Kim Daljin Art Research: 7 fig. 2, 31 fig. 9. Seoul Metropolitan Government: 8 fig. 3. Courtesy of the artist: 9 fig. 4, 19 fig. 5, 33 fig. 11, 59. Courtesy of the artist and Daejeon Museum of Art: 14–15. Courtesy of the author and the artist: 27 fig. 6. Hongik University Museum, Seoul © Lee Ufan: 29 fig. 7. Courtesy of Kukje Gallery: 29 fig. 8, 41 top. Courtesy of Park Seok-Won: 33 fig. 10. Courtesy of Powerlong Museum: 38–39. © Ha Chong-Hyun: 41 second from top, 41 third from top, 42 top, 43. © and courtesy of Kim Daljin Art Archives and Museum: 41 bottom, 42 middle. © Suh Seung-Won: 42 bottom. Courtesy of the artist and Kukje Gallery. Photo by Sangtae Kim: 46, 49, 51, 53, 55, 57, 69, 83, 84–85, 88–89, 100, 101, 102, 103. Courtesy of the artist and Kukje Gallery. Photo by Chunho Ahn: 47, 64–65, 68, 76–77, 80, 87, 90, 91, 92, 94, 95, 97, 99. Courtesy of the artist. Photo by Sangtae Kim: 53. Courtesy of the artist and Tina Kim Gallery. Photo by Chunho Ahn: 58, 93. Courtesy of the artist. Photo by Chunho Ahn: 61. Solomon R. Guggenheim Museum, New York. Gift, the Samsung Foundation of Culture, 2015: 62–63. Collection of Leeum, Samsung Museum of Art. Photo by Sangtae Kim: 66–67. Collection of MoMA. Gift of Glenn and Eva Dubin: 70–71. Collection of M+ Hong Kong. Courtesy of the artist and M+ Hong Kong: 73. The Art Institute of Chicago / Art Resource, NY: 74–75. Courtesy of the artist and Tina Kim Gallery. Photo by Sebastiano Pellion di Persano: 79, 81. Courtesy of the artist and Tina Kim Gallery. Photo by Dario Lasagni: 105. Courtesy of the artist and Tina Kim Gallery. Photo by Hyunjung Rhee: 107, 108–9. Courtesy of the artist and Kukje Gallery: 110–11. Giorgio Bombieri, Comune di Venezia: 122, 123, 128.

Cover: *Conjunction 21-74*, 2021. Oil on hemp cloth, 70 7/8 x 70 7/8 inches (180 x 180 cm). Courtesy of the artist and Kukje Gallery. Photo by Chunho Ahn.

This catalogue was published in conjunction with the exhibition
Ha Chong-Hyun, curated by Sunjung Kim
Collateral Event of the 59th International Art Exhibition—
La Biennale di Venezia
April 23–August 24, 2022
Palazzetto Tito (Istituzione Fondazione Bevilacqua La Masa;
Dorsoduro, 2826, 30123 Venezia VE, Italy)

Published by Gregory R. Miller & Co., New York, and Kukje Art and Culture Foundation, Seoul

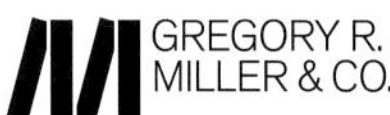

Gregory R. Miller & Co.
62 Cooper Square
New York, NY 10003
grmandco.com

KUKJE
ART & CULTURE FOUNDATION

54 Samcheong-ro
Jongno-gu Seoul
03053 Korea
www.kukjegallery.com

Essays edited by Nick Herman

Distributed worldwide by

ARTBOOK | D.A.P.
75 Broad Street, Suite 630
New York, NY 10013
artbook.com

ISBN 978-1-941366-48-6
Library of Congress Cataloging-in-Publication data on file with the publisher

EXHIBITION CREDITS
Curator: Sunjung Kim
Coordinators: Jiwoong Jeong, Stefano Coletto, Chiara Toso, Sooyoung Choi, Mikyung Lee, SoYoung Kim
Assistants: Claire Suhyoon Moon, Dabin Seo, Kendall Kim
PR: Third Eye, Heijeong Yoon, Joorhee Kwon, Seungmin Matilda Lee
Production: Tosetto Allestimenti

CATALOGUE CREDITS
Designed by Brette Richmond
Edited by SoYoung Kim and Ami Yang
Copy-edited by Natalie Danford

Color separations, printing, and binding by Conti Tipocolor, Florence Italy

Exhibition organized by Kukje Art and Culture Foundation and La Fondazione Bevilacqua La Masa

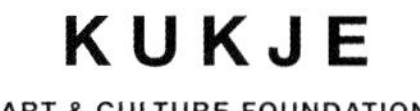

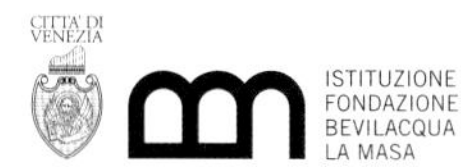

Publication sponsored by Kukje Gallery, Seoul; Tina Kim Gallery, New York; Almine Rech, Paris, Brussels, London, New York, Shanghai; Blum and Poe, Los Angeles, New York, Tokyo

KUKJE GALLERY   TINA KIM GALLERY   ALMINE RECH   BLUM & POE Los Angeles, New York, Tokyo

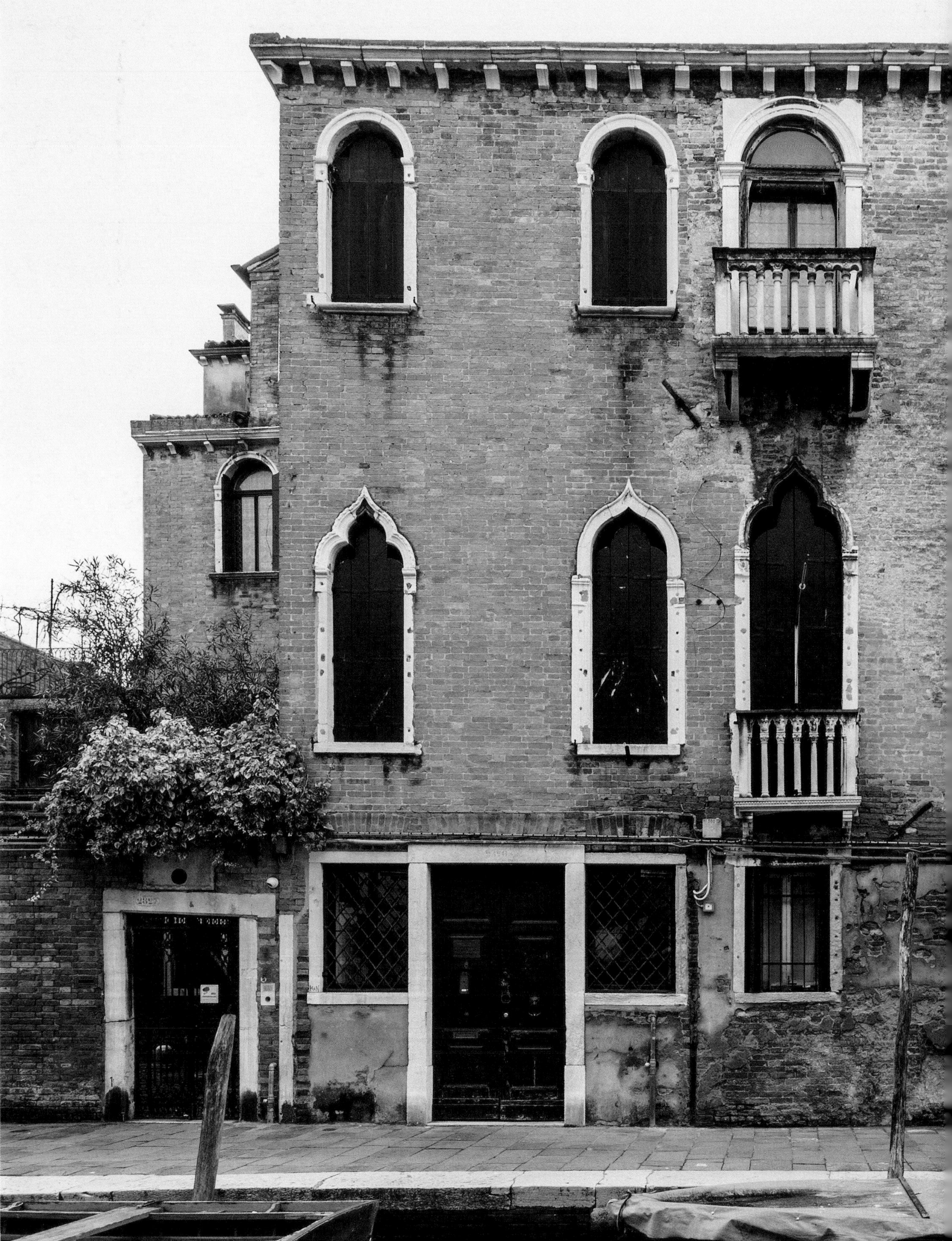